QUEEN VICTORIA

DAVID ROSS

WAVERLEY
BOOKS

Published 2023 by Waverley Books,
an imprint of The Gresham Publishing Company Ltd,
31, Six Harmony Row, Glasgow, G51 3BA, Scotland.

Copyright © 2019 The Gresham Publishing Company

First Published in 2019 by Geddes & Grosset. Reprinted 2023.

All rights reserved. No part of this publication may be reproduced, stored in a retrieval system, or transmitted, in any form or by any means, electronic, mechanical, photocopying, recording or otherwise without the prior permission of the copyright holder.

Conditions of Sale:

This book is sold with the condition that it will not, by way of trade or otherwise, be resold, hired out, lent, or otherwise distributed or circulated in any form or style of binding or cover other than that in which it is published and without the same conditions being imposed on the subsequent purchaser.

ISBN: 978-1-84934-506-4

Printed and bound in the EU.

Picture section credits:

The Illustrated London News: p2 (top), p3 (top left, bottom), p4 (top right, bottom left, bottom right), p5 (top);

Shutterstock: p2 (bottom, © Georgios Kollidas), p3 (top right, © Everett Historical), p8 (top, © Everett Historical);

Special Collections Toronto Public Library: p8 (bottom);

National Galleries of Scotland Commons: p7 (top);

Queen Victoria – Her Grand Life and Glorious Reign, (ed. J Coulter, 1901): p6;

Tallis's History and Description of the Crystal Palace (J Tallis & Co, 1852): p5 (bottom);

William Ewart Gladstone and his Contemporaries (Thomas Archer, 1883): p4 (top left).

CONTENTS

CHAPTER 1
The Making of a Queen — 5

CHAPTER 2
The Making of a Wife — 21

CHAPTER 3
The Making of a Mother — 50

CHAPTER 4
The Making of a Widow — 96

CHAPTER 5
The Making of an Empress — 134

Queen Victoria: Important Dates — 179

Select Bibliography — 192

All trades must be learned, and nowadays the trade of a *constitutional Sovereign, to do it well, is a very difficult one.*

> Leopold I, King of the Belgians,
> in a letter to Queen Victoria, 16 January 1838

CHAPTER 1

The Making of a Queen

Queen Victoria is Great Britain's second longest-reigning monarch, after Queen Elizabeth II, with sixty-four years between becoming queen in 1837 and her death in 1901. By the later years of her life, it was difficult for those around her to think that she had ever been young. But of course she had been a very young queen in 1837: only eighteen years old when she was awakened at six o'clock on the morning of 20 June, to be told by the Lord Chamberlain and the Archbishop of Canterbury, who knelt as she stood before them in her dressing-gown, that King William IV was dead and she was now Queen of the United Kingdom of Great Britain and Ireland.

Her accession to the throne was a posthumous triumph for her father, the Duke of Kent, who had died in 1820 before she was a year old. He was the fourth of King George III's seven sons. If one of the prime duties of a monarch is to provide amply for the succession, then George III was an exemplary king in that respect at least. When he died in 1820, only six days after the Duke of Kent, six of his sons and five daughters were still alive.

Victoria was born on 24 May 1819, and christened Alexandrina Victoria, after her godfather, the Tsar Alexander of Russia, and her mother, Victoria Maria Louisa. Her father had wished to call her Elizabeth but was overruled by his eldest brother, the Prince Regent, who felt that the queenly parallel was a piece of impertinence. Her birth and baptism excited little in the way of public interest. At the time, the royal family was held in something very close to contempt by most people. George III was eighty-two and had himself been King for sixty years. After periodic bouts of insanity, he had become permanently incapable from 1811, when his eldest son, later George IV, was made Regent. Old, mad, and blind, George III was an invisible figure shut up in Windsor Castle. The Regent, grossly corpulent ('Prinny has let loose his belly, which now reaches his knees,' wrote a waspish commentator, the courtier and politician Thomas Creevey), was a notorious debauchee, and his brothers were also held in varying degrees of public indifference or disesteem. Several were better known in Hanover – still also ruled by Britain's Hanoverian royal family – than in England. Because of the Hanover connection, the royal family was very much Anglo-German in its interests, speech, and marital links.

The royal offspring were less successful in sustaining the dynasty. The Regent had divorced his wife, and his daughter, Charlotte, had died in childbirth with her baby in 1817. The five daughters were childless or unmarried. The Duke of York, next in line to the throne, also had no children. The other sons had numerous children and grandchildren but none of these could possibly become king or queen since, under the Royal Marriages Act of the previous century, all were deemed illegitimate. Even if their fathers had entered into a form of marriage, it was of a morganatic sort, giving no official status to their wives, and of no account in terms of the succession.

When in 1818, after the death of Princess Charlotte, the Duke of Kent, aged fifty, came somewhat belatedly to look for a suitable official bride, he had long been in a liaison with a French-Canadian lady, Julie de Montgenet de St Laurent, and they had a son and daughter. His zeal to become the father of the heir presumptive to the British and Hanoverian thrones was not purely caused by a sense of duty. If he made a suitable marriage, he would be in a position to claim an official income, and though at £24,000 a year he was a rich man he, like his brothers, lived well beyond his means. The Duke made it known that he would consider ditching his companion of twenty-seven years and marrying a suitable German princess, if the government would provide him with £25,000 a year and pay off his debts.

In May 1818 he did marry Princess Victoria of Leiningen, daughter of the Duke of Saxe-Coburg. The best that the House of Commons – which controlled the public moneys – would do for him was £6000 a year, which greatly annoyed the Duke, though others were not surprised. Talking about Kent and his brothers, the Duke of Wellington remarked:

> 'They are the damnedest millstones about the necks of any Government that can be imagined. They have insulted – *personally* insulted – two-thirds of the gentlemen of England, and how can it be wondered at that they take their revenge of them in the House of Commons?'

The childbearing abilities of the Duke's new wife were not in doubt. She was thirty-two, and widow of the Prince of Leiningen: Germany at this time was still a patchwork of separate kingdoms and small semi-independent states each with its ruling family. She had two young children, Feodora and Charles. The family settled at the Leiningen home of Amorbach, and the Duchess duly became pregnant. Determined that the child should be born in England, Kent transported his wife and Feodora to London in time for the baby's birth. They were allotted rooms in Kensington Palace, and there the future queen was born. The baby was close enough to the succession for a number of dignitaries to be present in an adjacent room, to ensure no impostor-babe was smuggled in. They included the Archbishop of Canterbury and the Duke of Wellington. Perhaps the Duke of Kent would have preferred a boy, but it was said that a gypsy fortune-teller had told him he would have an only child and she would be a great queen. Hence perhaps his wish to give the name of England's greatest queen to the baby girl. The subsequent birth of a son would automatically have put him ahead of his elder sister in the succession. But a severe chill, caught in the Atlantic damps of Sidmouth, where the family had retired for the winter of 1819–20, ended the life of the Duke and left Victoria Louisa a widow once again.

With Kent's death clearly imminent, the Duchess sent for

her brother Leopold, who had been the husband of Princess Charlotte. He came accompanied by a German doctor, Christian Friedrich Stockmar. He could do nothing for the Duke, except that, as Leopold's trusted family counsellor as well as physician, he prompted the immediate writing of a will, which gave guardianship of the baby Victoria to her mother. Stockmar, then aged thirty-one, would continue to play an influential role behind the scenes for many years to come. Leopold, too, would be a key figure in the life of the fatherless young Princess. Aged twenty-nine when his niece was born, he had the resourcefulness and ambition that characterised the Saxe-Coburgs and made their obscure and unproductive German duchy into the nursery of European royalty in the nineteenth century.

Kent's elder brother, the Duke of Clarence, had also made a belated official marriage, and though his wife had produced a stillborn child, there remained a real possibility that a Clarence heir would yet be born and take precedence over the Duchess of Kent's infant daughter. The Duchess herself was ignored by the royal family. The Regent, now King George IV, was positively hostile and said he 'would be damned if he consented' to granting an annuity to her. He and his brothers had been irked by the popularity of Leopold in Britain. On the death of Charlotte, the Regent had been voted £50,000 a year by Parliament, something no Hanoverian ever got. In the end, Parliament allowed £6000 a year to the Duchess, and Leopold increased this by another £3000. In a Britain where the great majority of the population subsisted on a family income of less than £50 a year, this was substantial wealth, but compared with the landed nobility and the newly rich industrialists, who lived in vastly opulent style, it did not enable the Duchess of Kent to keep a large or lavish household. She was allowed to keep the rooms in Kensington Palace, and Leopold, with a shrewd eye on the future, prevailed on her to remain there and not to return to Germany, as she would have preferred.

It was thus in London, on the periphery of the court circle, in almost complete seclusion from the wider public, and in a domestic circle dominated by German ladies, that the young Princess had her home. Unlike the domestic life of George IV and his brothers, that of the Duchess of Kent was immensely respectable. The infant Victoria, always called Drina at this time, was very much its focal point. In later life, looking through the Duchess's possessions, Victoria would be touched to find just how much she had monopolised her mother's love and interest. The Duchess's lady-in-waiting, Baroness de Späth, and the Princess's nanny, Mrs Brock, were equally devoted, and the little girl, greatly indulged, developed a strong strain of wilfulness that was evidently part of her nature. In 1824, when she was five, an important new person entered her life. Fräulein Louise Lehzen had been governess to her half-sister, Feodora, and so was already well known to the Duchess. The daughter of a Lutheran pastor in Hanover, she was thirty years older than Victoria, a serious-minded and emotional woman, with little humour but enough intelligence and sensitivity to see that the way to win over the headstrong and tantrum-prone child was not through coercion but by winning her affection. This the governess, always known as 'Lehzen', successfully did, without sacrificing her authority, though initially she found her new charge the 'most passionate and naughty child' she had ever come across. On one occasion the child threw a pair of scissors at her governess. Though she learned to control it to a large degree, a quick temper was always close to the surface in Queen Victoria. But soon, despite the governess's insistence on lessons and good behaviour, she came to love Lehzen, and for thirteen years there was scarcely a day in which the two were not together. Another quality was noted in the young Princess, besides impetuosity: she was unfailingly honest, remarking much later that 'As a child, I never told a falsehood, though I knew I would be punished.'

Victoria's half-sister, Feodora, was a member of the household, but she was too old to be a playmate. Although, very occasionally, well-born little girls were brought to play,

Lehzen usually played with her charge as well as taught her. There was a large collection of dolls, with which Victoria played until she was fourteen, dressing them in different costumes and enacting scenes from history or stories. The secluded life with its regular routines and its familiar figures often seemed tedious, and she was always glad when there was a chance to visit her Uncle Leopold, at his house, Claremont, where life was more relaxed. Meetings with the King were rare. On one memorable occasion, when she was seven, she was invited with her mother and sister to Windsor. In his biography of Queen Victoria, Lytton Strachey described the scene:

> 'The old rip, bewigged and gouty, ornate and enormous, with his jewelled mistress by his side and his flaunting court about him, received the tiny creature who was one day to hold in those same halls a very different state. "Give me your little paw," he said; and two ages touched. Next morning, driving in his phaeton with the Duchess of Gloucester, he met the Duchess of Kent and her child in the park. "Pop her in" were his orders, which, to the terror of the mother and the delight of the daughter, were instantly obeyed. Off they dashed to Virginia Water, where there was a great barge, full of lords and ladies fishing, and another barge with a band ... the King turned to his small niece. "What is your favourite tune? The band shall play it." "God Save the King, sir," was the immediate answer. The Princess's reply has been praised as an early example of a tact which was afterwards famous. But she was a very truthful child, and perhaps it was her genuine opinion.'

Such happenings were rare, though among senior politicians and court officials it was becoming year by year more probable that the Duchess of Kent's daughter would, sooner or later, become queen. In 1830, George IV died and his brother, the Duke of Clarence, became King William IV. Clarence's aversion to the Saxe-Coburgs was just as great as his brothers' and, although it was plain that his queen, Adelaide, whose second child, Elizabeth, had died at three months, was most unlikely to produce an heir (he had ten children by the actress Mrs Jordan), he refused to recognise Princess Victoria as heir presumptive. Parliament, however, did and voted the Duchess an extra £10,000 a year, and gave her the status of Regent in the event of Victoria becoming queen while still under eighteen. She said it was the first happy day she had known for ten years. None of this was to William IV's liking. Eccentric, explosively tempered, often drunk, and totally devoid of social graces, he took what opportunities he could to offend and insult the Duchess of Kent. The Duchess responded in kind. Finding that Victoria was not to be given precedence over the King's younger brothers, her uncles, in the coronation procession, the Duchess, much to Victoria's mortification, refused to attend the ceremony at all.

In William IV's eyes, the Duchess's offence was not so much the fact that she had produced the heir to the throne, or even her much-resented refusal to acknowledge the numerous 'Fitzclarences' – his children by Mrs Jordan, who were regularly present at court – as the air of barely suppressed anticipation that was exuded from Kensington Palace. Despite the plain and socially secluded lifestyle of her establishment, and the ever-present need for economy, the Duchess harboured great expectations. Other expectations gathered around her too. Politically, the country was increasingly in a fever as the decade of the 1820s came to a close. Demand for the reform of Parliament had been growing. The Tories, who had been the dominant party for over forty years, found the ground moving under their feet. Nevertheless, many resisted the notion of reform, and few did so more doughtily than King William. From 1830 to 1832, with his strong and open encouragement, the House of Lords held out against the House of Commons' Reform Bill. Only when a general election in 1832 brought a huge Parliamentary majority for the Whigs did he finally accept the inevitable. The new Prime Minister, Charles Grey, obtained the King's reluctant agreement that, if the Lords still blocked reform, enough reformist Whigs would be given peerages to form a majority. The Duchess of Kent, though by no means a political animal, was associated with the Whigs, partly because her husband, rather surprisingly, had also shown sympathies towards Whig and even more radically minded politicians. With a Whig government in power, her significance and sense of self-importance increased. Cold-shouldered by the court, she had friends in a government that had taught both King and Lords an unpalatable lesson.

The young Princess had always known that she was somebody special. In an era when respect for social rank was automatic, to be the King's niece and daughter of a royal Duke set one apart, even as a child. When Victoria was twelve, it was finally imparted to her that she was almost certain to become queen on the death of her uncle. Until this point she had not known quite how special she was. Lehzen made the revelation, by showing her a genealogical table of her own family. The line that stemmed from George I, and, albeit with a few right-angled bends, from many kings and queens before him, back to Stuarts, Tudors, and Plantagenets – so many names from her history books – came to its current end in the person of Alexandrina Victoria. Her first recorded reaction was to say, 'I will be good.' Afterwards she wrote that 'I cried much on learning it.'

Now there was more coming and going, and important visitors conversing with the Duchess in her drawing room, but the daily routine of the child's life did not alter greatly. As she passed from girlhood into adolescence, however, she began to form certain views and opinions, even intentions, of her own. She had been a rather lonely little girl, despite the permanent presence of her mother and of Lehzen. Now she knew that the inscrutable power of destiny had set her apart from the rest of humanity for her entire life. The prospect must have appeared daunting, if also exciting and alluring.

Loneliness was not the same thing as being solitary. Victoria was never alone. Strachey recorded that up to the day of her accession, she never went downstairs without someone beside her holding her hand. She shared her mother's bedroom. Her days were spent with Lehzen, who had been rewarded for her services with a German title in 1827 and was now Baroness Lehzen. There was no place that Victoria could consider her own. Her education continued, with lessons in deportment and dancing. The Duchess of Northumberland, as official governess, supervised her tuition. She was best at languages, a valuable gift in one who would correspond with royal cousins in many European countries, and she could converse fluently in German, English, and French. She was no intellectual, and her tastes were always of a middlebrow sort. Clever people, apart from her husband, alarmed her, as did witty people, unless they also had the kind of personal charm to which she could respond.

Her sheltered upbringing and a sense of her station in life made her shy and reserved, and the reserve increased in her teenage years, when she found herself increasingly restive within the protective surroundings of her mother's household, and yet had to keep her thoughts to herself. Some, if not all, of those thoughts, could be confided to Lehzen; some could be written in the diary which she began to keep at the age of thirteen and which she maintained all through her life. The occasional relief of visits to Uncle Leopold at Claremont had stopped when she was eleven and he was placed on the throne of the newly formed kingdom of Belgium, where he could, and did, fulfil his own theories on the role of a constitutional monarch.

Protectiveness in the Kent household had another side to it. The people responsible for the nurturing of a future queen could hardly be expected not to think about what the future might hold for them. Chief among these was her mother. If King William, who was sixty-five in 1830 and not in good health, should die before Victoria came of age, then Victoria Louisa would become Regent. In effect she would be Queen. The powers, the influence, the wealth, the majesty currently endowed on the crusty, splenetic 'sailor king' would be in her keeping. But the time was not long. For royalty, the age of emancipation was eighteen, not twenty-one as it was for everyone else. Her daughter would come of age in 1837.

The Duchess's chief confidant was Captain John Conroy, Comptroller of her Household, who had been her husband's military equerry. If she dreamed of her role as Regent, he in turn intended to be the Regent's closest adviser. Conroy was of an Anglo-Irish family, with a wife and daughter; they, too, had rooms in Kensington Palace as part of the Kent suite. Malicious gossip suggested that Conroy and the Duchess were lovers but, though their relationship was close and confidential, this is most unlikely, not least because Conroy's wife was on the premises and the Duchess shared her bedroom with the Princess. Conroy was the only male influence in the Duchess of Kent's entourage, and his importance to her grew when her brother, Leopold, removed to Brussels. In 1830, the Duchess of Clarence, about to become Queen Adelaide, warned her sister-in-law in a letter that Conroy was making her cut herself off too much from the royal family.

> 'They believe that he tries to remove everything which might obstruct his influence, so that he may exercise his power *alone*, and alone, too, one day reap the fruits of his influence.'

The well-meant remonstrance simply encouraged the Duchess's hostility and pushed her into even more complicity with Conroy's arrangements and instructions. He succeeded first in convincing her that without him, George IV would take the young Victoria away from her mother's control and influence, and then that her uncle, the Duke of Cumberland, was plotting to poison his niece in order to become king himself. Conroy's 'Kensington System' decreed that the Princess should lead a quiet life and meet as few people as possible, especially boys. 'I long sadly for some gaiety' she confided to her diary.

He put forward his own daughter, Victoire, as the Princess's companion, but the Princess did not like her. A natural bully in an age when men were much more free to exercise such instincts, Conroy cultivated the mother but saw no reason to be other than his brusque and cutting self to the daughter. She came to detest him, and her mother, realising this, was puzzled. The Duchess turned to her old friend Stockmar in her perplexity at her daughter's failure to admire the Comptroller. Stockmar in his reply pointed out that the Princess might be resentful of 'what must have looked to her as an exercise of undue control over herself.'

The Duchess could not see it. She and Conroy failed completely to realise they were making a fundamental mistake, one which few people ever made after them and none with any success, and that was to take Victoria for granted. To them she was young, quiet, pious, and obedient. Her management seemed to present no great problem. When a long-standing lady-in-waiting, Baroness Späth, also remonstrated with the Duchess, she was sent packing. The Princess had a formidable ally in Lehzen, who was resolutely and implacably opposed to Conroy. As Lehzen was held in high regard by George IV and William IV after him, the Duchess dared not dismiss her, and so 'precious Lehzen' remained. Then in 1834 an additional lady-in-waiting was chosen by the Duchess, as a counter-balance to Lehzen. This was Lady Flora Hastings, described as 'a gaunt, sharp-tongued spinster' and intended to be an alternative companion to the Princess. Lady Flora, however, was far too evidently part of Sir John Conroy's scheme of things and she failed completely to gain Victoria's confidence. Indeed, the Princess greatly disliked her, and this was to have a disagreeable consequence in a few years' time.

In the autumn of 1835, as Victoria approached her fourteenth birthday, she became increasingly unwell and was unable to leave her room for five weeks. For most of the month of October she even gave up writing her diary because she felt so weak and listless. No clear diagnosis of her condition was made, and she seemed to exhibit such a range of symptoms as to baffle the doctors, from back pains, to loss of appetite, stiffness of the joints, and hair falling out. Conroy considered it 'whims', but used her weakness to try to make her sign a document appointing him her secretary. She refused, even when a pen was forced into her fingers. At one point, her illness led to delirium, but by the New Year, constantly tended by Lehzen, she recovered her former health. But for two years she was unable to indulge in a favourite pastime, that of riding.

Irked as William IV was by the sense of a 'queen-in-waiting', he did not blame the Princess, for whom he and Queen Adelaide had always had affection, but regarded her mother with a deep loathing, intensified when she and Conroy began a series of provincial tours with the young Victoria that took on an increasingly ceremonious tone. In August 1836 at a state banquet in Windsor to celebrate his birthday, the King's impatience completely gave way, and he rose to deliver a furious tirade against the Duchess of Kent. The immediate cause was her appropriation of seventeen rooms in Kensington Palace against his specific orders, but he poured out all his pent-up hostility. Complaining about the Duchess's insults to him, her evil advisers, and her keeping the Princess away from court life, he expressed the hope that his life might be prolonged by six months, to spare the country the calamity of a regency. The Duchess sat through it and preserved her dignity, while the Princess burst into tears. If the Duchess would have been pleased by William IV's death while her daughter was still a minor, the monarch was equally determined to thwart her ambition. Despite a serious illness when Victoria was seventeen, the King survived for the celebration of her coming of age in May 1837. To the intense anger of the Duchess, he provided the Princess with an allowance of £10,000 a year, specifically to be at her own disposal.

It was evident to all that William was weakening rapidly and could not have long to live. From his palace in Brussels, King Leopold wrote frequent letters to his niece. He was anxious to help prepare her for the role that would soon be hers.

Himself a constitutional monarch, his powers and duties clearly defined, he had a modern concept of kingship and wanted to impress it upon her.

> 'The business of the highest in a State, is certainly, in my opinion, to act with great impartiality and a spirit of justice for the good of all.'

In those last months of her uncle's reign, Leopold and Lehzen were important supporters of the young Victoria as the power struggle went on – a struggle she was only partly aware of at the time. But Leopold was far away, and her chief ally was Lehzen, whom she described in her diary in ever-more affectionate terms, to the extent of writing in her diary in 1838 of 'my ANGELIC dearest mother Lehzen, whom I do so love.'

The Duchess and Conroy had not given up the dream of a regency. They pressed the Princess continually and vehemently to accept Sir John (he had been given a Hanoverian knighthood in 1827) as her private secretary. They dwelt upon the difficult decisions, the immense responsibilities, and the arduous duties incumbent upon a reigning queen. She was so young, so inexperienced, and so shy. How much better it would be for her, if she would invite her loving mother to accept those tasks and responsibilities on her behalf. To others, they described Victoria in different terms, even as 'retarded'. The Duchess of Kent has generally been regarded as the dupe and tool of the ambitious and unscrupulous Conroy, who, though she did not know it, was also abusing his position as Controller of her finances. She was certainly deeply under his influence, but in her behaviour towards her daughter, her own will and judgement cannot be completely discounted. The Duchess, too, was ambitious.

Kept informed of what was going on by the alert and anxious Lehzen, Leopold sent Stockmar to London on 15 May 1837, and that shrewd diplomat very quickly sized up the situation. Writing to Leopold, he noted that the Princess was both calm and resolute, and determined to give away none of her rights.

Her relations with her mother had deteriorated, since the Duchess had allowed Conroy to 'insult the Princess in her presence' without reproaching him. 'O'Hum' was Stockmar's jocular code-name for Conroy, who was clearly getting more desperate as time went on. 'O'Hum continues the system of intimidation with the genius of a madman ... the Princess continues to refuse firmly to give her Mamma her promise that she will make O'Hum her confidential adviser.' In June, Conroy urged the Duchess to keep her daughter shut up until she had signed a paper appointing him her private secretary.

The government at the time, with the Whigs in power, was headed by Lord Melbourne. It was then the custom, on the death of the monarch, for the government to resign, and Leopold strongly urged his niece not only to retain Melbourne as her Prime Minister, but also to trust him absolutely. He would have come to London himself, to offer her guidance, but for a sense of delicacy, lest people might think a foreign king was interfering with the governing of Great Britain. William IV, now on his deathbed, also contrived to send a message commending Melbourne.

The King's end came at twelve minutes past two in the morning on 20 June 1837 in Windsor Castle. At that moment the sleeping Princess became Queen Victoria. It was almost six when the dignitaries roused the porter at Kensington Palace and brought her the news. Her mother woke her, but, as she noted that very day in her diary, Victoria saw the Archbishop and the Lord Chamberlain alone.

> 'Lord Conyngham then informed me that my poor Uncle, the King, was no more ... and consequently that I am *Queen* ... Since it has pleased Providence to place me in this station, I shall do my utmost to fulfil my duty towards my country; I am very young, and perhaps in many, though not all things, inexperienced, but I am sure, that very few have more real good will and more real desire to do what is fit and right than I have.'

She breakfasted with Stockmar that day, while Sir John and the Duchess were left to contemplate the failure of their scheme and the end of their dreams. At half past eight she wrote a brief letter to King Leopold, signing it as 'Your devoted and attached Niece, Victoria R'. She wrote also to Queen Adelaide, who replied that same day, as 'Your Majesty's most devoted Friend, Aunt and Subject'. At nine o'clock Lord Melbourne came to present the Queen with his condolences, his humble loyalty, and his resignation. Again she saw him alone, and immediately told him that it was her wish that he should continue to head her government. He kissed her hand and left, returning at eleven with a number of other Privy Councillors, for the first Council of the new reign. Strachey described the scene.

> 'The great assembly of lords and notables, bishops, generals, and Ministers of State, saw the doors thrown open and a very short, very slim girl in deep plain mourning come into the room alone and move forward to her seat with extraordinary dignity and grace; they saw a countenance, not beautiful, but prepossessing – fair hair, blue prominent eyes, a small curved nose, an open mouth revealing the upper teeth, a tiny chin, a clear complexion, and, over all, the strangely mingled signs of innocence, of gravity, of youth, and of composure; they heard a high unwavering voice reading aloud with perfect clarity; and then, the ceremony over, they saw the small figure rise and, with the same consummate grace, the same amazing dignity, pass out from among them, as she had come in, alone.

Victoria had begun her reign as she meant to continue. Her composure on this formidable occasion covered up a sense of insecurity that was chiefly the legacy of Conroy's and her mother's attempts to dominate her and to devalue her own judgement and abilities. But if she felt insecure, she did not feel inadequate. She had always been taught to see herself as special, and for six years she had known she was going to be queen. The lessons in deportment and movement had been well learned by a girl who also knew her station in life. Despite her short stature and increasing stoutness as the years wore on, she always retained this ability to move with grace and yet to hold a certain circumstantiality about her as though she breathed a different air. In a sense she did. No one was more profoundly aware than she was of the fact that she was different. However socially grand other persons might be, there were others who could call themselves their equals. She had no equal in her own country.

CHAPTER 2

The Making of a Wife

The British Constitution is famous for being non-existent. No single document has ever attempted to set out the precise manner in which the country is governed, and where individual responsibilities begin and end. This lack has been greatly praised and greatly deplored; it has been used both as a curb and a spur by politicians. But if there is no constitution, there is no shortage of constitutional practice, of precedents, of Acts of Parliament, of High Court judgments, and pronouncements by various persons as to what the rulers of the country might or might not do in almost any imaginable situation. In the long and eventful history of England, Scotland, Ireland, Wales, and Great Britain, there have been many developments and changes in the business and organisation of government. Compared to the monarchs of most countries, a British king or queen plays a relatively restricted role. He, or she, reigns but does not rule – the sovereign body in the country is Parliament. As the political writer Walter Bagehot, author of *The English Constitution*, jovially put it, the Queen, if required to do so by vote of Parliament, could be obliged to sign her own death warrant. Victoria had become, as she well knew, a constitutional monarch of limited powers. Her uncle, Leopold, had been an important tutor and example in this respect, particularly after his own installation as King of the Belgians.

And yet, the government was *her* government, invited by her to remain in office; the army and the navy were *her* army and navy. She was the head of two national Churches, both of a Protestant form but with great differences in their theology and methods of worship. She stood at the head of every great institution of the country, the guarantor of justice, the fount of honour. The person and function of the monarch gave legitimacy to every act of the state from the levying of taxes to the sentencing of criminals. It was in her name that even the post was delivered, through the Royal Mail.

William IV and George IV, like their father, had taken a direct part in politics, albeit one largely played behind the scenes. William's predilection for the Tories was undisguised, but he had not been able to withstand the popular support for the Whigs which had kept them as the governing party during the last years of his reign. But at least he had ensured the appointment of a conservatively minded member of that party, Lord Melbourne, as Prime Minister, rather than any of the more reformist Whigs, such as Lord John Russell. Partly in a continuation of the late Duke's views, partly in opposition to the court, the Duchess of Kent's household had always aligned itself with the Whigs, and of course its Whiggish sympathies were well known to the general public.

Though the monarchy held a pre-eminent place in national life, the public was perfectly capable of making a distinction between the institution and the person who embodied it. Few kings had been so widely despised as George IV. With William IV, there was little improvement: his violent temper, his eccentricities, and his large illegitimate family maintained at court, made him a figure of fun and an object of pious horror to the godly minded. The royal family had been an object of general contempt for sixty years or more. To the people of Britain, the new Queen's uncles and grandfather had been all too well known. She herself was an unknown quantity.

Victoria's youth, her fatherless childhood, perhaps also the fact that the Kents had been at a distance from the disreputable Windsor household, all combined to arouse public interest and sympathy in the girl who had inherited the crown. Unlike her Hanoverian predecessors, she was not also the monarch of Hanover. The German principality's Salic Law did not admit women to the throne, and her uncle – and heir presumptive – the Duke of Cumberland, acceded there. This only made Victoria seem more 'British' to her people. 'She looked so young, so innocent and good,' wrote the wife of the American

Ambassador, after a dinner at Buckingham Palace. She described the queen in some detail, as being of a size ...

> ' ... below the middle [in fact Victoria was scarcely five feet tall] but her figure is finely proportioned, and a little embonpoint. Her bust, like most English women's, is very good; hands and feet are small and very pretty. Her face, though not beautiful, has a look of spirituality, so bright and yet so tranquil that one feels voluntarily impressed with the idea that a good and pure spirit dwells within ... . Her eyes are blue, large, and full; her mouth, which is her worst feature, is generally a little open; her teeth small and short; and she shows her gums when she laughs, which is rather disfiguring.'

This plumpish, diminutive young person knew her own mind. She resolved to move to Buckingham Palace as early as possible; when told it could not be managed so soon, she replied that she would move in on 13 July and expected the necessary work to be complete by then. The work was done on time. A door was made to join her bedroom to Baroness Lehzen's room. The Duchess of Kent also moved to Buckingham Palace, but was installed in a small set of rooms at the other end from her daughter. Lehzen and Stockmar were Victoria's confidants and advisers. The Duchess felt so excluded that she presented Victoria with a copy of King Lear, Shakespeare's play about ungrateful daughters, for her nineteenth birthday.

Conroy was not allowed in the Queen's sight. The frustrated Comptroller now wished to retire from the Duchess's household, but not until his demands were met. These consisted of a peerage, the Grand Cross of the Order of the Bath, and a pension of £3000 a year from the Privy Purse. Lord Melbourne saw this as gross impudence, but to keep Conroy quiet, and as a gesture to the Duchess, agreed the very large pension and offered a baronetcy. This was not enough for Conroy, but he was finally induced to retire by the promise, which was never honoured, that he should be given an Irish peerage as soon as a vacancy arose. Conroy remained a bitter figure, ready to wreak mischief from the sidelines. The Duchess's efforts to plead for him, and at the same time to get her own debts paid off and her status as 'Queen Mother' officially acknowledged, further eroded her relations with the young Queen. There were unpleasant scenes when mother and daughter met, but this daughter had a trump card that she was not afraid to play. 'On one occasion,' she told Lord Melbourne, 'I was forced to remind her who I was.' 'Quite right. Disagreeable but necessary,' said Melbourne.

Victoria's first Prime Minister had very speedily become a close friend and ally. Aged fifty-eight in 1837, he was a politician of immense experience, and he settled very quickly into the role of paternal mentor to the young Queen, whose earnestness and eagerness to learn he found touching and endearing. His wife, the notorious Lady Caroline Lamb, who had been infatuated with the poet Lord Byron, had died in 1828, and his own private life had more kinship with the depraved days of the Regency than with the primness to come. But the Queen found him interesting rather than shocking. She relished his willingness to speak to her directly and honestly. Faced with a bewildering range of issues, causes, and claims on her attention, she was wholly reliant on him to point the way. Highly intelligent, widely read, and conservative by instinct, Melbourne had a melancholic but mellow humour; he had learned to look at life tolerantly but without much hope for its betterment. He was a prime example of the kind of English politician whose party affiliation was almost an accident; who drifted into positions of power without apparent effort; whose background of family wealth and classical education was not aristocratic but professional (his father, the first Lord Melbourne, was a successful lawyer).

Next in influence, though far behind, was Lord Palmerston, the Foreign Secretary, whose vast experience and ease with business impressed the Queen, though his ebulliently casual manner could be alarming. He, like Melbourne, taught her a lot about protocol as well as statecraft. When the Duke of Lucca was invited to dine by William IV, he had received a card. But the Duke felt that a personal note was the correct thing for an invitation to a sovereign prince, and when another royal invitation was likely, he made his views known. Palmerston advised the Queen to write a note, 'Your Majesty may think this is a small matter, but the Duke is a small Sovereign.' The Queen felt very much at ease with Melbourne and his administration; but nevertheless he was the leader of the Whigs, and inasmuch as she became dependent on his guidance, and almost as much so on his company, the young Queen was a Whig queen.

This did her no good with the Tories. Although not in power, they remained a force in the nation. Their greatest figure was the Duke of Wellington, ten years older than Melbourne but still with many active years ahead of him in 1837, but their political leader was Sir Robert Peel, who had been Prime Minister in 1834–35, and who was chiefly responsible for turning the old Tory party into the modern Conservative Party. Men such as Wellington and Peel treated the Queen with the greatest respect, but the Tory press was no respecter of persons, especially if they were Whigs.

In her diary on Christmas Day 1839, Victoria wrote of Melbourne as 'one whom I look up to as a father.' His remarks, his visits, his actions, take up a large part of the diary between 1837 and 1840. There were few days when they did not meet, and normally he would spend up to six hours a day with her. Official business in the morning would be followed by horse riding in the Park after lunch. He would return to dine with the Queen at eight and stay on until ten o'clock. His avuncular affection for her was plain, but it was also the affection of a tutor for a willing and clever pupil. For, despite her fondness for riding, for games and dances, she took her duties not only seriously but enthusiastically. When Lord Melbourne read her long despatches from Lord Durham, the Governor-General of Canada, first having explained the history of that colony, she listened with attention, and she attended assiduously to her papers.

> 'I have *so many* communications from the Ministers, and from me to them, and I get so many papers to sign every day, that I always have a *very great* deal to do. I *delight* in this work.'

Her own sense of propriety, and Melbourne's guidance, enabled her to tactfully head off her uncle, Leopold, who had written shortly after her accession to say that before she decided on anything important, 'I should be glad if you would consult me.' It may have been kindly meant, but the beloved uncle was also a foreign monarch, and it was not appropriate for the British Queen to seek the advice of the King of the Belgians. His frequent letters covered many subjects, but Leopold was anxious about the status and security of Belgium, and wanted to draw a message of support from the British government. Victoria, he suggested, might prompt her Ministers to abandon their policy of strict neutrality in his own difficulties with France and Holland. Her replies, though full of devoted sentiments, ignored his requests until finally she wrote, 'I see, with regret, that upon this one subject we cannot agree. I shall, therefore, limit myself to my expressions of very sincere wishes for the welfare and prosperity of Belgium.' With that, Leopold had to be content, and he was sensible enough to realise it, and to make no further requests of that nature, though he complained regularly about the British government's attitude. In due time, the Queen would have no hesitation about political interference, but it was never prompted by anything other than her own strong views. Of course, not everything that she had to deal with was of great political importance. Melbourne wrote her a note on 21 March 1838 about Lord Amelius Beauclerk, her first naval aide-de-camp, who …

> '… intended to ask an audience today of your Majesty, and that the object of it was to ask that he and the other Aides-de-Camp might wear sashes. This was always refused by the late King as being absurd and ridiculous

– as it is, particularly considering Lord Amelius's figure – and your Majesty had perhaps better say that you can make no change.'

The 'Kensington System' had ensured that Victoria knew very few other young people, and practically no boys at all. On a few occasions there had been visitors of her own age from the extensive tribe of her royal and ducal relations in the German principalities. When she was fourteen, her cousins, the Princes Alexander and Ernst of Württemberg came to stay, and were duly recorded in the diary: 'They are both extremely tall. Alexander is very handsome, and Ernst has a very kind expression. They are both EXTREMELY amiable.' When she was sixteen, she wrote at greater length about two further cousins, the sons of her mother's eldest brother, the Duke of Saxe-Coburg, who came with their father on a three-week visit. Ernest was almost eighteen and Albert was sixteen, three months younger than Victoria, but she wrote about them as if they were much older. They seemed to her to be more sophisticated, more educated, and more accomplished than she was.

> 'I sat between my dear cousins on the sofa and we looked at drawings. They both draw very well, particularly Albert, and are both exceedingly fond of music; they play very nicely on the piano. The more I see them the more I am delighted with them, and the more I love them ... they are quite an example for any young person.'

When they left, she described them as ...

> '... those *dearest* beloved cousins, whom I *do* love so VERY VERY dearly; *much more dearly* than any other cousins in the *world* .... They have both learnt a great deal, and are very clever, naturally clever, particularly Albert, who is the more reflecting of the two, and they

like very much talking about serious and instructive
things and yet are so *very very* merry and gay and
happy, like young people ought to be.'

A hint of wistfulness on the part of the sixteen-year-old Victoria is detectable here. There was not a lot of gaiety or happiness in her life; with the cousins gone, she was back to the company of Lehzen and her dog, Dash, of her mother and the detested Sir John.

Even though at Buckingham Palace she could, and did, give dinners – 'I have very pleasant large dinners every day,' she told Leopold in a letter of July 1837 – and dances, the years of seclusion had made her shy and incapable of easy small talk, something which continued throughout her life. Consciousness of her exalted rank accentuated this reserve, and most people found her a stiff and stilted conversationalist. But there was another side to the young Queen: she relished dancing, and romping with small children, and her sense of release and independence made her lighthearted within herself. She resumed riding as a daily enjoyment. Some outings were made incognito, to plays and the Opera, to avoid unnecessary formalities, but sometimes she was recognised: a not unpleasant experience for a young queen who enjoyed the public's esteem. The sharp-eyed old gossip Thomas Creevey noticed this aspect of 'little Vic', as he referred to her in his journal, when she paid a visit in 1838 to Brighton – once the favourite resort of her disreputable uncle, King George IV.

'A more homely little being you never beheld, *when she
is at her ease*, and she is evidently dying to be always
more so. She laughs in real earnest, opening her mouth
as wide as it can go, showing not very pretty gums … .
She blushes and laughs every instant in so natural a way
as to disarm anybody.'

With those whom she liked and trusted, the young Queen could be completely relaxed, but strangers and people in whom she sensed overfamiliarity or an air of condescension could encounter a glassy stare and chilly formality; it was not only her mother who had to remember who she was.

On 28 June 1838, Victoria was crowned at Westminster Abbey, in a grand, lengthy, and sometimes confused ceremony of which she recorded almost every detail. Although her coronation was 'a most beautiful and impressive moment', she confided to Melbourne afterwards that the crown had hurt her. He complimented her on her bearing and made her laugh with jokes about the pageboys and the bishops' copes. Afterwards there was a dinner, a small affair, for thirteen family members and Lords Melbourne and Surrey. She withdrew from the dinner at twenty past eleven, but then went to her mother's balcony, to watch, as an unseen spectator, the fireworks in Green Park.

Her circle of confidential friends was still a narrow one and consisted entirely of persons a good deal older than she was – Lehzen, Stockmar, and Melbourne. The favoured place of the two Germans in the royal household was well known, much discussed and disapproved of by many people in government and administrative circles. Melbourne, who heartily approved of both, had often to speak out in defence of their influence, which he regarded as good and positive, all the more so as they helped to keep the Duchess of Kent at bay.

However, none of these mature and intelligent people foresaw or could prevent the disastrous affair of Lady Flora Hastings, which brought Victoria's 'honeymoon' with the British public to an early and rancorous end. Lady Flora, with Sir John Conroy, remained a member of the Duchess of Kent's household and therefore part of the larger Buckingham Palace ménage. In the winter of 1838, Lady Flora, suffering from a stomach disorder, became quite plump, and the Queen and Lehzen leapt to the view that she was pregnant, with Sir John as the father. Such a charge, for which there was no evidence, could not be kept secret. Victoria hoped by exposing their relationship to get rid of two detested figures from her childhood.

By the end of January 1839, the two households under the same roof had become two enemy camps. Caught between the two, the royal doctor, Sir James Clark, without examining Lady Flora, told Melbourne he was 'reasonably sure' Lady Flora was pregnant. Lady Flora was asked to leave the Palace. She, her family, and the Duchess of Kent felt deeply insulted by the assumption so freely made by the Queen. Finally on 17 February, Lady Flora submitted to an examination that made it clear that far from being pregnant, she was a virgin. The Queen received Lady Flora, took her hand, kissed her and expressed her regrets. Then Clark and the colleague who had examined Lady Flora expressed some reservations about their own verdict. With Conroy doing his best to stir things up, and the Hastings family's sense of outrage, the whole story soon became public knowledge, with Lady Flora seen as the innocent victim of a slanderous plot that was intended to discredit the Duchess of Kent and her household. The Tory press took up the cause, with scornful attacks on Lehzen and Melbourne and heavy hints about the Queen's involvement. In early July, Lady Flora Hastings died, of what was diagnosed in a postmortem examination as a liver tumour. Victoria saw her, alone, a few days before her death, and noted in her diary that the patient seemed 'literally a skeleton, but the body very much swollen like a person who is with child'. There was no hint of contrition, but the Queen's diaries were heavily edited before being published after her death.

The posthumously established chastity of Lady Flora compounded the discredit of those who had conspired against her. The public cynicism about royalty returned. Moral victory was with the Duchess of Kent. 'The Queen's popularity,' wrote Charles Greville, Clerk to the Privy Council, 'has sunk to zero.'

The Hastings affair had its part to play in a larger political storm that blew up in the early summer of 1839. Its stresses had intensified the bonds between Victoria and her immediate retinue of aristocratic attendants, the Ladies of the Bedchamber. Unsurprisingly, these ladies were all from the

Whig aristocracy. But on 7 May, following a near defeat in the House of Commons, Melbourne's government felt obliged to resign. Victoria, already beset, was distraught at the thought of the Tories, whom she saw as outright enemies, forming a government. She had a particular dislike of Sir Robert Peel, who had none of Melbourne's ease of manner. On Melbourne's advice, she sent for the Duke of Wellington and asked him to form a government. He declined, saying he was too old, and advised her to send for Peel, which she reluctantly did. To form a minority administration was not easy at the best of times, and the Tory leader was well aware of the hostility and suspicion with which the Queen regarded him. The leading Tory paper, The Morning Post, was still full of anti-Palace diatribes. In the course of a difficult and tense interview, Peel expressed a desire that, with a Tory government, some at least of the Ladies of the Bedchamber should be supplied from the wives and daughters of his supporters. As the Ladies occupied a semi-official position, his request was reasonable. But the Queen saw it as a personal attack and blankly refused to make any changes at all. Even the Duke of Wellington could not make her budge. 'Is Sir Robert so weak that even the Ladies must be of his opinion?' she asked him. But Peel would not back down either. After much to-do, he informed her, with impeccable courtesy, that he was 'humbly returning into Your Majesty's hands the important trust which Your Majesty had been graciously pleased to commit to him.' She wasted no time in summoning Melbourne and inviting him to resume office, which he did. The twenty-year-old Whig Queen, through her intransigence, had saved her Whig government.

The Bedchamber business did her no harm with the public, and she herself felt she had triumphed. Stockmar, who was away in Germany, saw more clearly that she had overreached herself and that in future the politicians would ensure that the royal powers were more confined. Melbourne, who guessed that the Tories would soon be elected to power, tried his best to reconcile her to Peel, with little success. The Duke of Wellington performed a service for her when he finally persuaded Sir John Conroy to retire.

Looking back, the mature Victoria was not proud of her first years as Queen. Perhaps the paternal Melbourne, for all that he taught her, also indulged her wilfulness too much. Some of her utterances at the time suggest she was playing a role in her own imagination. 'The Queen of England will not submit to such trickery. Keep yourself in readiness for you may soon be wanted,' she wrote to Melbourne about Peel's demand. She burned much of her correspondence from this time, and blamed 'that life of constant amusement, flattery, excitement, and mere politics' for its bad effect on her own 'naturally simple and serious nature'. But, as she added in a note to Sir Theodore Martin in 1869, 'all changed in 1840.'

Though his efforts to influence British foreign policy had failed, Uncle Leopold had by no means ceased to give advice to his niece, and to plan for her future. As the senior member in rank of the House of Coburg, he felt very strongly for the family's welfare and advancement. Almost since the births of Victoria and Albert, he and his mother had contemplated the thought of a marriage between the two cousins. Leopold was by no means the only person to plan for Victoria's marriage, but as head of the family, he was in a very strong position. As he watched his nephew grow to manhood, he came to the view that he was indeed in all respects the ideal husband for Victoria. The Coburg visit to London of 1836 had had a serious dynastic purpose, as the two seventeen-year-olds well knew. But the girl had not made up her mind. In July 1839 she wrote to her uncle.

> 'I am anxious that you should acquaint Uncle Ernest [Albert's father] that if I should like Albert, that I can make *no final promise this year*, for, at the very earliest, any such event could not take place till *two or three years hence*. For, independent of my youth, and my great repugnance to change my present position, there is no anxiety evinced in this country for such an event, and it

would be more prudent, in my opinion, to wait till some such demonstration is shown, – else if it were hurried it might produce discontent.'

This was in anticipation of a new visit from the Coburg cousins, which took place in October 1839. But with the arrival of Albert, all her reservations vanished. Three days after his arrival, she told Melbourne that she had 'a good deal changed her opinion as to marrying'; two days after that, on 15 October, she called her cousin to a private meeting in Windsor Castle, and told him it would make her too happy if he would consent to what she wished. They embraced 'over and over again'. After the long years of preparation, and after all the doubts, it had been a genuine, and a whirlwind, romance.

Melbourne had approved the match, but without great enthusiasm. Uncle Leopold was told immediately, in secret; the Duchess of Kent not until 10 November. Even the servants knew by then. Nothing could better indicate the gulf between daughter and mother. The whole thing had come about with such speed that many observers thought that Victoria had secretly planned it without telling the Prime Minister. In fact her motives in accelerating her marriage, the greatest event of her personal life, were complex. At the time, she was feeling isolated and insecure. The Hastings affair had shaken her, and 'her' government's grasp on power was shaky. She had discovered that being Queen was not all adulation and parties. Lehzen was by her side, as always, but she was not the ideal emotional confidante. Albert was still as intelligent and knowledgeable as on his first visit, still a skilled performer on the piano, but he was no longer a teenager. His English was greatly improved, and in his demeanour, in the tenderness of his attentions to her, it was clear that he had become a man. He was German – with none of the odium of the French or the problems of being British. He was of the family – this counted for a lot. They already shared a great deal. He was strong, reliable, discreet, and she knew him to be a person of integrity just as she knew his father, Duke Ernest, to be a worthless rake. It was a short time in which to discover all his talents, but, when she went wholeheartedly for something, Victoria did not indulge in half measures. The official announcement was made on 23 November, and aroused mixed reactions. Some commentators feared the genetic consequences of a marriage between first cousins. Others sneered at Albert's motives, as the impoverished state – relatively speaking – of the Coburgs was well known.

> 'He comes to take for better or for worse
> England's fat Queen and England's fatter purse.'

Albert was not in love, and was somewhat astonished to become the object of such intense devotion. A conscientious Coburg, very much influenced by Leopold I, and perhaps even more by Stockmar, who had been a sort of tutor-chaperone to him, he played his part manfully. 'My future lot is high and brilliant, but plentifully strewn with thorns,' he wrote to a close friend. It was not all plain sailing for him. Britain was a foreign land, its political system unfamiliar to one used to small despotisms – the mysteries of its non-existent constitution seemed endless and baffling. As Queen, Victoria had many people, from the Prime Minister and the Lord Chamberlain down, who were ready to explain to her what her position required, and how to do it. There had been no husband of a reigning queen since Prince George of Denmark, Queen Anne's husband, more than a century before. George had been an undemanding, soldierly sort; Albert was very different. But there was no one to explain what the Consort's job was, because there was no such job.

In the months of their engagement, during which they corresponded daily, this did not matter greatly. Albert returned to Germany while Victoria struggled to have his status properly established. She floated the suggestion of 'King Consort' as an honorary title, to have it firmly rejected; he would be His Royal

Highness, the Prince Albert. A reigning king could endow his wife with majesty, a reigning queen, it seemed, could not do the same for her husband. The Prince had to have a 'Household' of immediate courtiers of his own, but despite his protests, he was allowed scant choice in its members. Woundingly to the Queen, Parliament voted him an income of £30,000 a year: an amount equivalent to the annual revenue of Coburg, but less than the £50,000 former royal consorts had received. She held Peel and the Tories responsible for what she saw as an insult. Ominously for Albert, his fiancée wrote to him telling him the arrangements she and her government were making for him were necessary, 'my dearest and most excellent Albert ... for your own good.' With his own notions of what his own good required, Albert was persuaded by Stockmar to bide his time. A lack of enthusiasm for the Coburg marriage was by no means restricted to the Tories, but Victoria seized on them as the chief opponents of Albert, to the point where she initially refused to invite their leaders to her wedding. The Duke of Wellington was to her 'an old Rebel' and it was only with great difficulty that Melbourne persuaded her that to exclude the Tory leaders would have a disastrous effect on national political life. Albert arrived for the wedding in a somewhat depressed frame of mind, with a substantial baggage of grievances and intentions.

On 10 February 1840, the pair were married in the Chapel Royal. Victoria promised to obey her husband, but the marriage ceremony, she knew, invoked a Power greater than Her Britannic Majesty, before which the grandest personages on earth were merely men and women. It was as a woman, not as a queen, that she made her marriage vows, and intended to keep them.

She had given more thought to what her husband would not do, than to what he should do, in his capacity as Consort. At this time, royal dukes were accustomed to taking part in debates and votes in the House of Lords, and to speaking their minds. It was clear to Victoria and to Melbourne that Albert should not be given a British ducal title, in case he made speeches in Parliament that might embarrass the Queen by showing a difference of opinion in the royal couple. Albert therefore had not even the diversion of a seat in the Lords. The Queen continued to see her ministers as before, alone. A life of luxurious idleness offered itself to Albert, but idleness was not part of his nature. He needed to be industrious. There were other difficulties, also. For almost as long as Victoria could remember, Lehzen had been there, as governess, supporter, and adviser. But Lehzen's role had expanded with Victoria's accession. She was the Keeper of the Queen's finances and, without any formal title, controlled the affairs of the royal household both at Buckingham Palace and at Windsor. As a loyal Coburg retainer, she had been a supporter of the marriage to Albert, but saw no reason to relinquish any of her responsibilities or to adapt her special relationship with the Queen. Like many another person wielding power behind the scenes, she had come to consider herself indispensable.

Victoria would not have disagreed; Lehzen's removal at this time would have been a terrible blow. In some important ways, the Queen was still very much in the mould of her Hanoverian forebears. More earnest than they had been, more conscious of duty, and far less improvident, she did not question the ramshackle array of custom, tradition, and habit that determined how her household was run. She had affairs of state to consider and ceremonial duties to perform. To find time for riding and entertainment was almost impossible when there was hardly time to examine the systems and hierarchies which ensured, somehow, that dinners were cooked and served, rooms prepared and cleaned, furniture repaired or regilded. More to the point, she was not interested. She still loved parties, and dancing, and staying up very late, a style of living that harked back to – if in a very much paler and seemlier version – the rackety times of her uncles, George IV and William IV. Her husband had grown up in a minor court where money had always been short and where economies were vital; he had been to university and understood something of political economy and the abstract philosophy beloved by German professors.

On a more personal level, he abhorred late nights, was bored by parties, and found it hard to fit in with the established pattern of court life. He enjoyed meetings and discussions with men of intellect and ideas, and such people both bored and alarmed his wife. His manner with other people was stiff and formal, and, like Victoria herself, he has been described by biographers as shy. Albert's stiffness and reserve were as much the products of assertive pride (he knew some of his wife's relations considered him insufficiently grand as a match), a feeling of alienation in a strange land, and his lack of a meaningful role in British life, as of any natural shyness. Even when his place was far more assured, he never lost that sense of distance.

The first years of married life were thus not without occasional troubles and tears. Albert's sense of frustration at his exclusion from Victoria's involvement with the business of government was all the sharper because he had strong views on how her role should be exercised, and he did not consider that his wife was doing it properly. His great support in this period was Stockmar, who still stood to him somewhat in the relation of tutor to pupil. From his privileged position behind the scenes, the Baron had studied British politics and government for long enough to realise that the structure was sufficiently open and flexible to offer ample scope for someone in Albert's position and of Albert's abilities, if he would be patient, firm, and – not least – appear supportive and appreciative of the British way, rather than present the air of an interfering German who wanted to change things. 'Magnanimity' was Stockmar's word: his pupil must struggle to keep the larger aim in view and not to give way to petty slights or the increasingly malicious attitude of Lehzen.

A rift had opened between Stockmar and his old ally, the Baroness. He saw her influence in the Queen's reluctance to discuss affairs of state with her husband, but Lehzen seemed immovable. Stockmar could talk to his political friends, however, like Melbourne, to whom he expressed the view that 'The Queen has not started upon a right principle. She should by degrees impart everything to him [Albert], but there is danger in his wishing it all at once.' In the long run, Victoria's attitude towards her husband was however the crucial element. She loved him, openly and demonstratively, and relished the pleasures of the marriage bed. Albert had access to the Queen of quite a different order to that of the old governess. In a short time, Victoria found herself to be pregnant. This was not a welcome discovery to her. Although she enjoyed the physical aspects of sexual love, she resented and bemoaned each of her numerous pregnancies and especially this first one, so soon after the wedding. Later she described the first two years of her marriage as 'utterly spoiled' by successive pregnancies.

A trial more often reserved for heads of state came on 10 June 1840 in the first attempt on her life, when she and Albert were driving down Constitution Hill in an open carriage. They were on the way to visit the Duchess of Kent, who had removed from Kensington Palace to Belgrave Square after her daughter's marriage. A shot was fired from the crowd, and Albert hastily pushed Victoria down, though not before she saw her assailant take aim at her for a second shot. The motives of the gunman, Edward Oxford, were never clearly established, though there were dark suggestions that the Queen's Uncle Ernest, now King of Hanover, was behind it. Until Victoria's child should be born, he was heir presumptive to the British throne. Oxford was charged with treason and found 'guilty but insane', and a new wave of popularity surged about the young Queen, who had borne herself with great courage and composure.

One result of the assassination attempt was the first official acknowledgement of Albert's growing acceptance. Government and Opposition both agreed that, in the event of the Queen dying but her child surviving, the Prince should be named Regent. Their first child, Victoria, known as 'the Princess Royal', was born on 21 November 1840. Uncle Leopold, in his letter of congratulation, was prophetic when he wrote that 'you will be a delighted and delightful Maman au milieu d'une belle et nombreuse famille' – though his niece responded a little tartly about 'the great inconvenience a large family would be to us all, and particularly to the country, independent of the hardship and inconvenience to myself; men never think, or at least seldom think, what a hard task it is for us women to go through this very often.' Perhaps it was her awareness of fulfilling what was usually a masculine role in addition to the burdens of pregnancy and motherhood that made her so averse to 'the trials which we poor women must go through'. Her second child, Albert Edward, was born less than a year later, on 9 November 1841, after a difficult and painful labour. As a boy, he took precedence over his sister; young as she was, the Queen now had an heir apparent.

Queen Victoria was unsentimental about new babies. She thought them froglike and had little interest in her own or her daughters' offspring until they acquired a few 'human' characteristics. Breastfeeding, like pregnancy, she considered a gross imposition, but it at least could be passed on to a wet nurse. Her feeling against breastfeeding was very strong: she regarded it with what she called an 'insurmountable disgust'.

Victoria was a woman of strong feelings and often found it impossible to hold them in check. Her temper frequently exploded, even against the beloved Albert, though in his case such tempests were followed by tears of regret and peacemaking. Most of the time he maintained his stiff magnanimity, but serious trouble broke out over the management of the royal children's nursery. The Queen was happy enough to leave this to Lehzen, Mrs Southey, the children's nurse, and the dubious professional talents of Sir James Clark. Albert, with a modern-minded penchant for fresh air and plain fare, deplored the overheated, frowsty atmosphere of the nursery rooms and suspected that the children were over-doctored and given too much rich food. In almost every quarrel he had given way, sometimes moved by, or hiding behind, a fear that Victoria's rages would lead her into a George III-like insanity. But in this matter he was determined to assert himself, and he succeeded, with Stockmar's aid.

The Baron was also invaluable in supporting him against Lehzen. Albert, frustrated and powerless, wrote that 'all the disagreeableness I suffer comes from one and the same person and that is precisely the person whom Victoria chooses for her friend and confidante.' Victoria, who also greatly valued and respected Stockmar, was shocked when the Baron said that he would withdraw from the royal household if Lehzen did not retire. By September 1842 she was finally persuaded that the time had come for Lehzen to go. The ex-governess was not an old woman – only fifty-eight – and might have hoped for many more years of power, but she withdrew without complaint from her place at the centre of the royal family to live with her sister in Bückeburg, close to Hanover. The Queen rewarded her well, with a pension and a carriage, but very soon she herself was acknowledging that to have kept the Baroness on had been a mistake. Though she continued to think affectionately of Lehzen, she also began to realise how much the Baroness had been belittling and misrepresenting Albert. She did not miss Lehzen – her husband was there, to more than fill the gap.

Albert had already proved his value to her in what once would have been a major crisis. Melbourne's government had staved off defeat in Parliament for a couple of years, but a defeat on a motion of confidence forced him to hold a general election in the summer of 1841. As he had expected, the Tories were victorious and nothing could rescue the Queen from the invidious task of having to ask Sir Robert Peel to form a government. To his credit, Melbourne had tried to prepare the Queen for the likelihood of a Tory majority, but the key figure in heading off anything like a new 'Bedchamber' crisis was the Prince. He believed that the Crown should be above the unseemly strife of politics, and with the two great political groupings both firmly loyal to the monarchy, saw that Victoria's open Whig bias was alienating her from a large section of the country, including many of the aristocracy and landed gentry. He was horrified to find that Lehzen was using the Privy Purse to subsidise Whig candidates. Through his Private

Secretary, George Anson, Albert established contact both with Melbourne and Peel, and it was arranged and agreed that, if the Tories should form a government, the Queen would 'procure the resignations of any ladies whom Sir Robert might object to.' Thus faces were saved on both sides, and though it was a long time before the Queen came to appreciate the qualities of Peel – a far greater statesman than Melbourne, but much less genial and urbane, and not nearly so good at making her feel at ease – the transition of government was effected with a minimum of royal resistance, and she behaved with courtesy, if not warmth, at their regular meetings, to someone whom she had characterised to Melbourne as 'that bad man Peel'.

The fact that Peel and Albert got on very well with each other also influenced her views. By the second half of 1842, after some eighteen difficult months, there was no doubt that Victoria had lost whatever battle had been going on between herself and Albert. But it is probably a great mistake to describe the event in those terms. Albert, after all, had been an unknown quantity to her. They had scarcely met before their marriage, which, despite her proposal, certainly had a strong element of arrangement about it. She was Queen, with a genuine and profound sense of duty and responsibility, which she felt, at first, was impossible to share with anyone. (Sir John Conroy was not forgotten.) Although the idea would never have been put into words, Albert had to not only prove himself capable of dominating her, but also to show himself worthy of her trust by playing a praiseworthy part in public life, before she would grant that trust, or even allow such a role. Fortified by Stockmar's encouragements, by the appreciation of such men as Melbourne, Peel, and Wellington, and by the tact of his Private Secretary, Anson, Albert achieved this. In this, as in other cases, once Victoria was convinced, her conversion was total and wholehearted, all the more so as this man was already her domestic 'dear Angel', the husband of her bosom and the father of her children. From then on, Albert would play an increasingly large part in royal business and national politics and eventually take a discreetly masked dominant role in this area. In 1852, the Queen could write that 'Lord Derby came to Albert at half past three, and Albert called me in at a little after four.' It was no social or incidental visit: Lord Derby was the incoming Prime Minister, come to present his plans for government.

Albert's 'emergence' initiated a new era in Victoria's life. But it took some time for this to become an established fact. Despite the installation of a Conservative ministry, she continued to correspond with Melbourne, and to ask and act on his advice. In this, the ex-premier was more to blame than she: he knew that proper practice meant that she should confine herself to advice from her ministers. But he was old, affectionate, and aware that he would never again lead a government. The Queen's desire for his continued company and counsel was too tempting to be resisted. A wide range of appointments was constantly being made in the Queen's name, from ambassadors to bishops, from army officers to regius professors. Although the names emanated from the Prime Minister's and other government offices, she had to sign their Letters Patent or commissions, and she was entitled to query the candidates' suitability and to put forward her own suggestions. During 1841–42 her own suggestions were usually prompted by Melbourne. It was Stockmar and Anson, with Albert anxious in the background, who eventually put a stop to this – by putting pressure on a grumpy and reluctant Melbourne to give up writing to the Queen on political affairs. As with Lehzen, Victoria was not upset by the withdrawal of Melbourne from public life. She now had her counsellor by her side, night and day. If Albert approved, she approved; if Albert frowned or shook his head, she disapproved.

Nonetheless, Victoria was not the conventional 'little woman' whose whole demeanour and set of opinions were subservient to her husband's. She was a person of strong character with a deep consciousness of her own unique status and responsibility. Lady Lyttelton, who had succeeded the unsatisfactory Mrs Southey as royal governess, observed that 'a vein of iron runs through her most extraordinary character.' If Albert had been a good-natured, indolent sportsman, she might have loved him no less, but she would not have regretted his absence from the council chamber. If he had been a political schemer out to subvert the British way of doing things, or of views too extreme to be acceptable, he would never have been admitted to it. But Albert was neither of these things. His concept of duty and service was as high as her own, and she came to fully accept his guiding rule, that in a constitutional monarchy, the Crown must not descend into the political arena. There was more than high-mindedness in this view. As some of his critics observed, Albert's aim was the stability of the Crown, not that of the country, and it certainly did not prevent the court from interfering in the political process.

As a child, Victoria had been lonely and, while still hardly more than a child, had been placed in an exalted but in some ways even more solitary situation. With her undoubtedly imperious strain went a deep sense of uncertainty and a need for reassurance and support. Albert resolved the uncertainties and provided the reassurance and support. In some ways it was as if he were ten years older rather than the same age as she was. She had lived by the moment and for herself, but he had a clear view of what their family life should be and how it should be lived. And so, for two decades of happy marriage, the partnership of Victoria-and-Albert was formed and maintained. Rereading her diary of only three years before, with its fulsome praise of Lord Melbourne, she made and initialled an addition in the margin.

> 'Reading this again, I cannot forbear remarking what
> an artificial sort of happiness *mine* was *then*, and what
> a blessing it is I have now in my beloved Husband
> *real* and solid happiness, which no Politics, no worldly
> reverses, *can* change; it could not have lasted long as
> it was then, for after all, kind and excellent as Lord M.
> is, and kind as he was to me, it was but in Society that I

had amusement, and I was only living on that superficial resource, which I *then fancied* was happiness! Thank God! For *me* and others, this is changed, and I *know what* REAL *happiness* is – V.R.'

In the autumn of 1842, another kind of new horizon opened for Victoria. For the first time, the Queen of England made the acquaintance of her realm of Scotland. She and Albert travelled by sea to Leith, disembarking there just as Mary I of Scotland had done on her return to Edinburgh in 1560. A keen reader of Sir Walter Scott, Victoria was pleased to feel that Stuart blood ran in her veins, from that remote ancestress, Sophie, daughter of James II and great-granddaughter of Mary Queen of Scots, who had married an Elector of Hanover. Their visit took them into the Highlands: 'The Highlands and the mountains are too beautiful, and we must come back for longer another time,' she wrote to Melbourne.

Despite the demands of state, home, and family – with Windsor replacing Buckingham Palace as the principal base – the Queen enjoyed travel. Unlike Albert, she was a good sailor and liked shipboard life. Peel's government provided for the construction of a royal yacht, the steamer Victoria and Albert, to enable her to make state visits in suitable style. The vessel was launched in April 1843 and in August made its maiden voyage along the south coast. By that time Victoria had already become accustomed to travel by train, her first journey having been made on 23 June 1842, from Slough to London (Windsor did not yet have a railway station). The Great Western and London & North Western railways built special carriages for royal journeys, but while the royal yacht was maintained at government expense, the railway companies charged the Queen's household for her travel. Though always somewhat nervous of trains, and insisting that hers should never exceed forty miles an hour, the Queen found the railway a highly convenient and restful form of travel. It was also a secluded one.

A second attempt on her life had happened in May 1842.

On 29 May, as she and Albert were driving back to Buckingham Palace from the Chapel Royal, and just as he was observing 'how civil the people were', they both saw a man point a pistol at their carriage. He was not apprehended. The following day the Queen set out for another drive, to Hampstead and back, with the deliberate intention of giving the man a chance to try again. Two equerries rode close to her and many plain-clothes police were distributed along the route. A gun was fired and a man was seized. His name was John Francis, and, like Oxford, a motive for assassination was never uncovered. He pleaded insanity but was condemned to hang. The sentence was subsequently changed to transportation for life, because of doubt as to whether his pistol had been loaded. Only two days after Francis's attempt, one John Bean shot at the Queen from a London crowd. It turned out that his pistol had been loaded only with paper and tobacco: he was probably a deranged attention-seeker rather than an assassin. But the authorities, and Prince Albert, were seriously concerned. An attack on the Queen's person was treason, and a treason trial was a cumbersome, complicated affair intended to deal with rebellious lords rather than street ruffians. In a few days, an Act was passed making an attempt on the Queen's life a high misdemeanour. Bean was sentenced to eighteen months in prison. The Queen seemed unperturbed by these events. Such acts of random violence were viewed philosophically by her as a professional hazard in the modern world. 'I was really not at all frightened,' she wrote to Leopold. At the time there was considerable political unrest among the working and country people of Britain, and intense activity on the part of the government and police to monitor and repress it, but none of the attacks on the Queen could be pinned on Chartists or Republicans or indeed any kind of semi-organised group.

During the decades of her reign, coal, iron and steam-driven machinery would make Britain immensely rich, the richest country in the world, and the most powerful. In the early 1840s, that trend was already well under way, with industrialisation on a scale never seen before. The population was increasing at an unprecedented rate. More people than ever before were rich, and far more than ever before were abjectly poor. The gulf between rich and poor was steadily widening. What was happening was beyond the control and understanding of any government. Among the few men who believed they understood what was going on were Karl Marx, who in 1849 would take refuge in London from political persecution in Germany, and his friend, Friedrich Engels, already making the social observations that would result in The Condition of the Working Classes in England in 1844, and in his co-authorship with Marx of The Communist Manifesto in 1848. Neither of these men would ever make the acquaintance of Queen Victoria, nor would she become familiar with their ideas. Naturally enough, she abhorred any suggestion of socialism or communism, tainted as they were for her with revolution and anti-monarchism.

Queen Victoria was the richest woman in England. Apart from the income of the royal estates, Parliament had voted her £328,000 a year to maintain the royal household (a sum which, incidentally, did not alter throughout her reign). Albert had taught her that she must be above politics. In as far as he held political opinions, they were mildly liberal in matters of superficial social improvement and reform, but firmly conservative about the fundamentals. She came to share his views, and both of them were also imbued with the feeling, more common in those days than it is now, that social rank and distinction, and its concomitants of wealth, prestige, and power to command service from others, were given by God and should be accepted as such, and, with due thanks and humility, exercised as such. While the Queen consented to become patron of some of the new charitable organisations, such as the one dedicated to making it illegal to employ 'climbing boys' in the chimney-sweeping trade, she felt no call to attempt to cure the deeper social evils of the country. Foreign affairs, the international prestige of Great Britain, and the problems and fates of continental royal families interested Victoria far more than the profound changes taking place within her four realms of England, Wales, Scotland and Ireland.

For Albert, however, one aspect of reform was closely related to home. He had been aghast from the start at the slipshod and unregulated way in which the royal household was run, but while Lehzen still ruled, had been unable to act. Several great mansions were Crown properties, including Kensington Palace where Victoria had grown up, but the Queen's two homes were Buckingham Palace and Windsor Castle. Both had undergone alterations and extensions under successive monarchs, but, in an age beginning to fully understand matters of hygiene and public health, they were old-fashioned, insanitary, and ill-adapted to the requirements of a youthful and rapidly growing family. The administration and accounting of both establishments were chaotic. Stockmar in 1841 produced for the Prince a vast document describing, as far as it could be understood, the current workings of the 'State of the Royal Household'. It revealed a jumble of conflicting roles between the Lord Chamberlain, the Lord Steward, and the Master of the Horse – three aristocratic functionaries, and their hierarchies of staff. These noblemen did not live at court and exercised little control. Inside Buckingham Palace, as Strachey recorded, it was believed that the kitchens and pantries were controlled by the Lord Steward, and the other rooms by the Chamberlain, but the footmen and other liveried staff were in the domain of the Master of the Horse.

> 'Naturally, in these circumstances the service was extremely defective and the lack of discipline among the servants disgraceful. They absented themselves for as long as they pleased and whenever the fancy took them; "And if," as the Baron put it "smoking, drinking, and other irregularities occur in the dormitories, where footmen, etc., sleep ten and twelve in each room, no one can help it." As for Her Majesty's guests, there was nobody to show them to their rooms, and they

were often left, having utterly lost their way in the complicated passages, to wander helpless by the hour. The strange division of authority extended not only to persons but also to things. The Queen observed that there was never a fire in the dining room. She enquired why. The answer was, "The Lord Steward lays the fire, and the Lord Chamberlain lights it"; the underlings of these two great noblemen having failed to come to an accommodation, there was no help for it – the Queen must eat in the cold.'

On one occasion, the French Prime Minister, Monsieur Guizot, a guest at Windsor in 1844, looking for his own room, found himself in the Queen's dressing room while she was having her hair brushed.

Inevitably, such confusion led to a great amount of embezzlement, fraud, and petty theft. During the first three months of 1840, it was reckoned that more than 24,000 dinners were served 'below stairs' at Buckingham Palace: more than 260 a day to a staff that certainly numbered less than half of the total. Purchasing was uncontrolled and corruption was rife. On a more sinister level, the lack of effective management led to a lack of security. Twice at least a strange youth – 'with a most repulsive appearance' and known as 'the boy Jones' – had simply climbed the wall and walked into the Palace. In November 1840, he was found hiding under a sofa in a room next to the Queen's bedroom, and declared that he had been skulking in the Palace for three days. Foreshadowing the latter-day habit of 'stalking' celebrities, Jones persisted in returning to loiter about the Palace after brief spells of imprisonment, until the authorities seized him and pressed him into the Royal Navy.

In 1844, with the Queen's support, Albert finally got to grips with this tangle of vested interests, supposed ancient custom, incompetence, and chicanery. Many people were paid for doing nothing; a famous example was the weekly charge of thirty-five shillings on 'Red Room Wine'. It was discovered that in George III's time, this room in Windsor Castle, with red hangings, had been used as a guardroom, and that five shillings a day had been provided for the officers' wine. The Red Room had long since lost this function and the guards were no more, but the money was paid regularly to an army officer, retired on half-pay, who held the position of under-butler but who did no work whatsoever.

At Stockmar's suggestion, a Master of the Household was appointed, with authority and responsibility for the administration of both Palace and Castle, and matters improved considerably, though total reform was impossible. As Peel remarked, 'Ancient usages are half the essence of royalty in England.' At this time, as readers of Dickens's novels will know well, the royal household was by no means unique among British state institutions in its decrepit and corrupt condition. The Prince was upbraided by those who lost their perquisites, sinecures, and opportunities for peculation, and by radical journalists who attacked his excessive thriftiness as readily as they would have condemned his extravagance, but he gained further respect among political leaders, as a man who could get things done.

However, the royal pair were not content with reforming their official dwellings. Palace and Castle were still, as tradition demanded, open house to a wide range of visitors. Much of the royal day was spent in semi-public activity. Guests at meals were an almost permanent feature of life. The Prince Regent's old retreat at Brighton, the Pavilion, was now at the centre of a busy resort and on their visits there the Queen and the Prince felt unpleasantly exposed to the interest of the crowd. Albert disliked too much society and wanted to make a home somewhere that would be a private refuge from the formalities and exposure of the court.

CHAPTER 3

The Making of a Mother

Victoria, who so disliked the physical indignities, stresses, and demands of pregnancy and motherhood, was to bear and bring up nine children. Of these, seven were born in the first ten years of her marriage. Her time from 1840 to the early 1850s, from the age of twenty-one into her thirties, was inevitably dominated by successive pregnancies. Princess Alice was born on 23 April 1843; Prince Albert on 6 August 1844; Princess Helena ('Lenchen') on 25 May 1846; Princess Louise on 1 May 1848; Prince Arthur on 1 May 1850. After a pause, Prince Leopold was born on 7 April 1853, and her last child, Princess Beatrice, was born on 14 April 1857.

The Queen's own memories of her childhood were not particularly pleasant ones, though one of the many things for which she felt grateful to Albert was the reconciliation he had brought about between her and her mother. The Duchess of Kent, who was of course Albert's aunt as well as his mother-in-law, had settled down to become 'a dear old lady' (as her ladies-in-waiting described her). Past rancours were forgotten on both sides, and she became a much-loved grandmother to the royal brood. Albert by contrast had happy memories of a childhood spent largely in the open air, scrambling about on forested hillsides with his brother. Both were determined to be exemplary parents, and they were united in the view that to be brought up at court as the centre of attention, in an atmosphere of formality and perpetual public exposure, was a very bad thing for a child. This was one of the things that prompted them to look for a private home. Occasional stays *en famille* at King Leopold's English house, Claremont, and once at Walmer Castle in Kent, had shown them how delightful seclusion from official life could be. In 1844, the Queen wrote from Claremont to her uncle:

'We leave dear Claremont, as usual, with the greatest regret; we are so peaceable here; Windsor is beautiful and comfortable, but it is a *palace*, and God knows *how willingly* I would always live with my beloved Albert and our children in the quiet and retirement of private life, and not be the constant object of observation, and of newspaper articles.'

In 1845, with the approval and encouragement of Peel, who was Prime Minister, the Queen bought the old house and estate of Osborne, on the Isle of Wight. The house was demolished and a new residence, designed by Albert and the builder, Thomas Cubitt, arose in its place. By 1846, they were able to move into its central portion, known as 'the Pavilion'. At last their desire to have a house in which they could live a private family life was fulfilled. The railway took them to Gosport, and they proceeded from there by boat to the island. Both inside and out, Osborne was very largely Albert's creation. Though grand, it was a country house and not a palace, intended for family use and not for state events. The locality reminded Albert both of Naples and of his old family home at Rosenau in Coburg, for which he had a strong sentimental regard, and these were the prime influences. The design of the house was Italianate and inspired a great many others in similar mode. The terrace, from which they could look out across the sea towards Gosport and Portsmouth, was modelled on that of the house at Rosenau. Over the years both house and grounds were extended until the estate reached over two thousand acres. Not all was decorative parkland: Albert laid out farms and made sure that they paid their way. Within the house, innumerable entwined V&A motifs displayed the unity of the royal couple. 'How happy we are here,' wrote the Queen in July 1849, ' ... never do I enjoy myself more, or more peacefully, than when I can be so much with my beloved Albert and follow him everywhere.' In earlier years, she had taken little interest in gardening or in natural history; now she was delighted to walk through the gardens and improved grounds of Osborne, while

Albert showed where he would plant his trees and shrubs, or explained to her the botanical names and qualities of the flowers and plants. Her admiration of Albert was by now so extreme and unqualified that it was a rapture to her simply to hear his earnest voice expound his unlimited knowledge, to see the enthusiasm in his mild eyes, to reflect that this paragon was her husband.

By that time, the pleasures of having a private home had been so amply proved that Victoria had in effect acquired a second one. In 1844, she had made her second visit to Scotland, sailing on the Victoria and Albert to Dundee, and travelling from there to Blair Atholl where the royal couple stayed in the castle as the guests of Lord and Lady Glenlyon. The Queen had been eager to return to Scotland, and was not disappointed. Once again she felt a sense of kinship with, almost a passion for, the Highlands. Albert, too, was happy there, reminded of his beloved Coburg by the conifer-clad hills, the turreted castles, the stags' head decorations and the deerstalking. But Victoria's feelings were deeper, almost turning into an exaltation. She was impressed not only by the scenery but by the people. She loved the Highlanders. 'They never make difficulties, but are cheerful, and happy, and merry, and ready to walk, and run, and do anything.' She and Albert both appreciated 'the good breeding, simplicity, and intelligence, which make it so pleasant and even instructive to talk to them.' On the return to Windsor she wrote in her diary that 'I cannot reconcile myself to be here again, and pine for my dear Highlands, the hills, the pure air, the quiet, the retirement, the liberty – all – more than is right.'

On the next visit, in 1847, it rained all the time but Victoria was not in the least put off. She felt she must keep a link with this region that meant so much to her, and in 1848 she took a lease on Balmoral House, a secluded laird's dwelling far up the River Dee, in fine countryside and on the 'dry' side of the Grampian massif. She bought the lease without even seeing the property, but their first visit confirmed that Balmoral offered everything they could wish for. In 1852, she bought it outright. While it was politic, and encouraged warm feelings towards the Queen among the Scots that she should have a house in Scotland, it was not done for these reasons. It was the Highlands with which she was besotted – not Scotland; the Highlanders, not the Scots. She thought Edinburgh a fine city, but not to stay in. The Palace of Holyroodhouse saw her only on infrequent occasions.

Perhaps she and Albert did not appreciate the degree of social change implied by their successful attempt to live their own lives to some extent at least. It showed a significant change in the British monarchy's perception of itself, and it led to a change in how the royal family itself was seen. In 1838, Uncle Leopold had written to her of the 'trade' of the constitutional monarch, and though it was as near as Leopold could come to a jest, it had a serious edge. Even though the Hanoverian monarchy's style was always more relaxed and informal than say, that of the Stuarts, or of the kings of France and Spain, it had still been regal and public. The kings lived at the centre of things, with a wide range of courtiers and attendants, and their accessibility, if only to a limited range of people, was taken for granted. It was an unprecedented and unique action for a reigning monarch, in full possession of her faculties, to remove herself from the court for extended periods, and live the life of a country gentlewoman. Many monarchs of the time would not have dared to do so, for fear of a coup in their absence; others, like the Austrian and Russian emperors, were too involved in government, for they ruled rather than reigned over their countries. The year of the Queen's first visit to Balmoral, 1848, was a year of exceptional turmoil in Europe. There was a revolution in Paris, where the Second Republic was declared, and another in Vienna, from where the great imperial minister, Count Metternich, fled to the security of London, along with the deposed French king, Louis-Philippe, and Prince William of Prussia. Across the continent, governments were shaken. Britain was not immune to unrest, but far from revolution; the Queen wrote to Leopold in February with some complacency that 'Our little riots are mere nothing, and the feeling here is good.' Queen Victoria took her 'trade' with immense seriousness, but she made a distinction between the person of the sovereign and the person of Alexandrina Victoria, wife and mother. Like a successful shopkeeper moving from rooms above the shop to a villa on the outskirts of town, but still making regular appearances behind the counter, she effected the notion that the monarch was an individual with a private life as well as an emblematic personage, the head of state. In this she set the pattern for her successors.

Not that the Isle of Wight and Highland sojourns were wholly cut off from official business. Like the shopkeeper wanting to see the daily accounts, the Queen required to be kept in touch with what was going on. This meant a constant flow of dispatch boxes and letters, but it also meant that senior ministers and other functionaries had to appear in person at Osborne and Balmoral. At least Osborne was only some three or four hours from London, but Balmoral meant a journey of a day and a night. And the house was small – only a poky little guest room was available for a visiting politician.

The royal parents took a close interest in their children, to a greater degree than many aristocratic families. Between 1842 and 1850 the governess in charge was Lady Lyttelton, a mild-natured woman who was loved by all. She was succeeded by Miss Sarah Hildyard, an equally loved figure, and a woman of learning and intellect, who remained until 1865. The tone of the nursery was however set by the Prince and the Queen, both of whom believed strongly in the possibility of 'moulding' their children to become exemplary characters. While naturally they expected the children to become part of the stratum of inter-related royal families that stretched from Madrid to St Petersburg, they took care that they should learn some quite basic skills. The girls were given cookery lessons, and each child had its own plot, and garden tools, at Osborne. Fears expressed by those who knew something of genetics at the time of Victoria's marriage seemed groundless – the royal children were patently not idiots.

Inevitably, the pattern of upbringing was set with the first two,

Victoria the Princess Royal, known to the family as 'Vicky', and Albert Edward, his mother's heir, known as 'Bertie'. They had little resemblance in character. Vicky was a highly intelligent child, a natural linguist who could speak English, French, and German before she was three years old, and a precocious reader whose appetite for learning delighted both parents but especially the Prince. Bertie was entirely different in this respect. Though in later life he was a competent linguist, he had no apparent urge to learn anything, and this seriously worried Albert, who took his responsibility as father of the future king with even more than his usual gravity and earnestness. He and Victoria could not forget that some notably dissolute figures were among this often sullen and unbiddable boy's recent ancestors. Lady Lyttelton said of him, aged five, that he was 'uncommonly averse to learning'.

All the children appeared to have inherited their mother's temper, and tantrums were frequent. Determined to exercise control, and to teach restraint, Albert occasionally beat them, encouraged by Victoria, who tended to consider him insufficiently severe in this respect, while he confided to Lord Clarendon that he thought her excessively harsh. Despite her bitter memories of the Kensington System, she imposed something rather similar on Bertie, in her anxiety that he would encounter unsuitable acquaintances. Stockmar, aged sixty-one in 1848 and still very much a counsellor to the Coburgs, encouraged this, emphasising that the young prince should be surrounded only by those who were 'good and pure'. In 1849, Bertie was given a tutor, the Rev Henry Birch, who immediately noticed that the segregated, hothouse flower treatment and the intense pressure of parental attention, were having an adverse effect, but Albert was unmoved. Birch was replaced in 1852 by Frederick Gibbs, and Bertie, now eleven, was subjected to a seven-hour schoolday, six days a week. Every moment of his waking time was prescribed for, and every moment was supposed to be dedicated to something worthy, or useful. Even when he tried hard, Bertie's best was never good enough for Albert, and he rarely tried at all. He suffered from unfavourable comparison with his brilliant elder sister as well as with his father's exalted standards.

His mother was no less critical. She had hoped for an eldest son in Albert's image, and instead it was increasingly apparent, as Bertie became an adolescent, that her worst fears were being realised and that he was cast in the image of George IV and the other reprobate Hanoverian great-uncles. He even – as she herself also did – looked like them. 'Handsome I cannot think him,' she wrote in a mood of exasperation in 1858, 'with that painfully small and narrow head, those immense features and total want of chin.' Rather dangerously, she wished for him that 'I only hope he will meet with some severe lesson to shame him out of his ignorance and dullness.'

If Bertie was the prime sufferer, all the royal children experienced similar efforts to ensure that their characters were moulded in the right way. Much later in life, Princess Louise commented on the practice of trying to enforce patterns of thought and behaviour on children, 'It was deplorable. I know, because I suffered from it.' But the Queen and the Prince were not just a Mrs and Mr Gradgrind [from Hard Times by Charles Dickens]. Although they happened more often when the children were young, there were many happy days in the nursery and both parents enjoyed playing with the children. The children were encouraged to talk and to express opinions. Albert had a toy fort built at Osborne, though probably a utilitarian aim was at the bottom of it, since Prince Arthur was specifically intended to become a soldier. Fortunately, this suited his own inclinations perfectly. On the whole, the children seem to have responded quite robustly to the parental moulding process. After Vicky had married the Crown Prince of Prussia, her mother reminded her in a letter of some former times.

> 'A more insubordinate and unequal-tempered child and girl I think I never saw! ... The trouble you gave us all was indeed very great.'

Perhaps, if the parents had been less demanding, the children would have been less insubordinate. The girls were cleverer and sparkier than the boys, except for Leopold, the second youngest, who was a studious child resembling his father in appearance and in other ways. Despite this, he was not his mother's favourite. Arthur, whom the Queen adored '... from the day of his birth. He has never given us a day's sorrow or trouble', occupied that position. Leopold was naughtier and more insubordinate. But from an early age he gave far greater cause for concern. He was a sickly child and it very soon became apparent that he suffered from haemophilia.

This condition, in which the blood lacks the normal clotting agents, was little understood in the mid-nineteenth century. It is a hereditary ailment, normally passed on through the female line but with the defective gene affecting only male offspring. There had been no known previous cases among Victoria's forebears, but as the number of her grandsons and great-grandsons spread, there were numerous haemophiliacs among them, including most famously the Tsarevitch of Russia, shot dead with his parents, sisters and other relations in 1918. The Queen fussed protectively over Leopold even more than over the other children.

Her maternal instinct was strong, but it was also strongly possessive. Her relationships with her children as they grew older will be looked at in a later chapter, but the pattern was set in their early childhoods. Far into their adult years, she would ply her children with instructions, medical advice, and unasked-for comments on their activities. She would unabashedly complain to one of them – especially Vicky – about the shortcomings of another – especially Bertie. But none were spared. It was a curious inversion of roles. Victoria used her family life to escape from the obligations of sovereignty, but within that sheltered context she ruled her nine children absolutely. She had established her own independence very firmly at the age of eighteen, but found it impossible to concede the same to her own children. Though her children showed a degree of understanding and forgiveness, she was not a good mother, being too critical, possessive, unimaginative and undemonstrative towards them.

By 1850, the mid-century mark, she had been twelve years on the throne. No longer a novelty, or even a young queen, for to be past thirty at that time was to be entering middle age, she had become a fixture in people's minds. The Queen and Prince Albert were, in general, popular and esteemed. The respectability of the royal family could not have been greater. Albert was a model of correct behaviour. He drank little, did not gamble, and had a strong dislike for the racier, gamier element in upper-class English life. He had no extramarital affairs and greatly disapproved of people who did. In his time, and for many years after it, no divorced woman – however guiltless – was ever received at Victoria's court. The events, or non-events, of 1848, and the steady increase of Indian territory under direct British rule, confirmed the sense that Britain was a stable monarchy at home and a world power, indeed the principal world power, abroad. A sense of increased national importance and confidence enhanced the dignity, and increased the formality and protocol, of court life. In the not so distant past, Britain had suffered indignities. The American colonies had been lost under Victoria's grandfather. The final victory over Napoleon, achieved with the help of Prussia, had been, as the Duke of Wellington still remembered, a close-run thing. Now, in the second decade of Victoria's reign, though there were troubles and problems aplenty to deal with, there seemed to be no task too great for Great Britain to undertake successfully.

There was a problem area which lay very close to home, however, and that was Ireland. Since 1801, there had been no Irish Parliament and the United Kingdom of Great Britain and Ireland had been established, with a hundred Irish members in the House of Commons. Ireland remained an overwhelmingly Roman Catholic country, with a fluctuating but never absent movement for the reinstatement of Home Rule. Between 1846 and 1848 it had gone through the travails of the Great Hunger, when the rural population, especially of the west and southwest, had been ravaged by starvation and disease. In a country of eight million people, a million died and between 1846 and 1850 a further million emigrated to the United States or Britain. In 1848, there had been a failed attempt at armed rebellion. A visit by the Queen to Ireland had, rather surprisingly, been considered in 1846. She wrote to Lord John Russell, who had become Prime Minister that year, expressing wariness on two counts.

> 'It is a journey which one day or other must be undertaken, and which the Queen would be glad to have accomplished, because it must be disagreeable to her that people should speculate whether she dare visit one part of her dominions. Much will depend on the proper moment ... when undertaken, it should be a National thing ... . As this is not a journey of pleasure like the Queen's former ones, but a State act, it will have to be done with a certain degree of State, and ought to be done handsomely. It cannot be expected that the main expense of it should fall upon the Civil List, nor would this be able to bear it.'

The state visit was eventually made in August 1849. Carefully managed by the authorities, it was an undoubted success. Travelling on the Victoria and Albert, the royal party of Queen, Prince and the four elder children visited Cobh (renamed Queenstown in her honour), Cork, Waterford, Dublin, and Belfast. Large crowds received the Queen with enthusiasm, and the government was pleased and relieved. Victoria kept a sharp eye on the scene, and reported to King Leopold from Dublin.

> 'The most perfect order was kept in spite of the immense mass of people assembled, and a more good-humoured crowd I never saw, but noisy and excitable

beyond belief, talking, jumping and shrieking instead of cheering .... You see more ragged and wretched people here than I ever saw anywhere else. *En revanche*, the women are really very handsome – quite in the lowest class – as well at Cork as here; such beautiful black eyes and hair and such fine colours and teeth.'

The Queen, however, did not take Ireland to her heart as she had the Highlands; there was not the same sense of kinship and belonging. Her duty had been done: she had dared, and triumphed, but she would only make two more visits there, widely separated in time.

The business of Ireland, however, was inseparable from English politics. Time and again during Victoria's reign and later, the difficulties of legislating for Ireland within the British context were to bring down governments and cause bitter political splits. Hostility in his own Tory party to Peel's Irish policy almost destroyed his government in 1845 and in 1846 when, largely in response to the Irish famine catastrophe, he won the struggle to repeal the Corn Laws, Tory rebels finally brought his government down, and Lord John Russell formed a Liberal administration. The Queen was almost as distraught at losing Peel as premier as she had been with Melbourne's going. Albert, too, was greatly disappointed. He had been an ardent and – somewhat against his own tenet – public supporter of the repeal of the Corn Laws; as an economic liberal he was a firm believer in Free Trade. In January 1846, he attended, as an observer, the House of Commons when Peel introduced the repeal motion, and was fiercely criticised by the Tory leader, Lord George Bentinck. Referring to 'that illustrious and royal personage who, as he stands nearest, is so justly dearest to Her who sits upon the throne', Bentinck accused Albert ...

' ... of allowing himself to be seduced by the First Minister of the Crown, to come down to this House to usher in, to give éclat, and, as it were, by reflection from the Queen, to give the semblance of a personal sanction of Her Majesty to a measure, which, be it for good or evil, a great majority of the landed aristocracy of England, of Scotland, and of Ireland, imagine fraught with deep injury, if not ruin ... .'

Bentinck was quite right: the oligarchic power of the landed aristocracy was something Albert deplored; and they, in return, disliked and mistrusted him. But he realised he had overstepped a mark, and that the attack was in fact a veiled one on the Queen herself. Albert did not attend a Commons debate again, and though by now he was fully involved in the affairs of the state, he confined his political activity to confidential and private contacts. He also ensured that despite their mutual disappointment in Peel's defeat, proper and effective relations were established with Russell and his cabinet, whose Parliamentary supremacy was confirmed by winning a general election in 1847.

The return of a Liberal government brought the sixty-two-year-old Lord Palmerston back as Foreign Secretary, his third time in that post. He had been second only to Melbourne as a tutor and mentor in Victoria's first years as Queen, and they had got on well. Now, however, she had Albert at her side. And behind the royal pair was Baron Stockmar, the trusted counsellor of the Coburgs, and a man well versed in the affairs of Europe. Palmerston saw a wider world than the cockpit of Europe, with its insecure royal dynasties, its fragile republics, and its many nationalities. Considering himself, with some reason, as of just as much consequence as the Prime Minister, he was determined to rule his department of state in his own way, and to his own policies. Inevitably this led to sharp disagreement between him and the royal couple. During the tumult of 1848, the Queen and Albert were affronted to find that their Foreign Secretary appeared to be aiding and encouraging the revolutionary movements that were tossing kings and princes from their thrones.

Foreign policy, especially towards Europe, was supposedly

a field in which the Queen should have considerable say, if only because the European monarchs, mostly with far more dictatorial powers than she herself had, were often her relatives and wrote personally to her. Her replies were always made with the cooperation and approval of the British government; and her own views were always the product of thoughtful consideration. Albert was even more rigorous in this respect. He found it natural and essential to examine every side of a complicated question carefully, writing down the salient points, and using the process of reasoned thinking to come to a careful and logical conclusion. Palmerston made his decisions on the instant and appeared to base them on no fixed principles at all. Worse, he acted without reference to the Queen. Lytton Strachey observed:

> 'Important Foreign Office despatches were either submitted to the Queen so late that there was no time to correct them, or they were not submitted to her at all; or, having been submitted, and some passage in them being objected to and an alteration suggested, they were after all sent off in their original form. The Queen complained; the Prince complained; both complained together. It was quite useless. Palmerston was most apologetic – could not understand how it had occurred – must give the clerks a wigging – certainly Her Majesty's wishes should be attended to, and such a thing should never happen again. But of course, it very soon happened again, and the royal remonstrance was redoubled.'

Lord John Russell was constantly complained to, but the impetuous Palmerston tended to treat his Prime Minister as he treated his Queen. Unfortunately for Russell, Queen and Prince, Palmerston's actions and personality went down very well with the public, and despite all the pressure from Windsor, he could not simply be sacked or transferred against his will to another post. The Queen's old warmth to him disappeared entirely. A chilly note despatched from Buckingham Palace on 17 February 1850 stated her attitude.

> 'Lord Palmerston has a perfect right to state to the Queen his reasons for disagreeing with her views, and will always have found her ready to listen to his reasons; but she cannot allow a servant of the Crown and her Minister to act contrary to her orders, and this without her knowledge.'

At this time, Palmerston was taking a high-handed line with Greece, a piece of 'gunboat diplomacy' in support of claims made by a Gibraltarian, Don Pacifico, against the Greek government. This modest matter seemed likely to cause a war. As usual, the Queen's comments were being ignored. Had either side chosen to take a public stance, a major constitutional crisis over the Queen's powers would have blown up. Instead the matter seethed in private meetings and memoranda. The intense exasperation felt by Victoria and Albert was increased by the fact that they had their own policy towards Germany, which Palmerston did not share. This was to promote the claim of Prussia to become the leading state in a Germanic Confederation. Naturally, they had a great concern for Germany, where so many of their relatives were rulers, while 'Pilgerstein', as they Germanised his name, cared nothing for the German principalities and seemed to have no system or coherent set of foreign policy ideas other than to promote British interests in a manner which Albert thought demeaned Britain and reduced the country's reputation among foreign governments and peoples. On 25 June 1850, Palmerston triumphantly survived a censure motion in the House of Commons, trouncing his critics in a speech lasting for over four hours, and became even more strongly entrenched than before. At this time, the Queen was also greatly distressed by the death of Peel, following a riding accident. Melbourne had died in 1848, so she had lost her two most trusted statesmen. Wellington was over eighty and very shaky – only the now-detested Palmerston seemed to be as hale and hearty, and disobedient, as ever.

The Queen had to endure almost two more years of being a helpless spectator of a foreign policy that was often repugnant to her and frequently seemed dangerous, though in fact Britain engaged in no war during this period. But finally the Foreign Secretary over-reached himself. On 2 December 1851, Louis-Napoleon Bonaparte, the Prince-President of France, staged a coup d'état, installing himself as Emperor and suspending the Parliamentary constitution. Despite the desire of the Queen, and of the Cabinet, to remain neutral and refrain from comment, Palmerston indicated his support for the coup. Russell had no option but to require the Foreign Secretary's resignation, which was reluctantly given on 20 December, in time to brighten the Christmas celebrations of the Queen and the Prince. Victoria felt emboldened to demand of the Prime Minister the absolute and unfettered right to approve or veto any candidate for the vacant post, now and hereafter, and her own nominee, Earl Granville, was duly appointed. But the royal couple had not seen the last of the irrepressible Palmerston.

During this phase of frustration and annoyance, if Victoria could seek some solace by visiting the nursery and inspecting the placid infant Prince Arthur, or by troubling Miss Hildyard about the progress and behaviour of the older children, she could also derive real pleasure from seeing her husband fully engaged, as his qualities merited, in a whole range of different activities. He was always with her when important questions were discussed, and took part in the discussions; afterwards, when the Minister or counsellors had withdrawn, he was still with her, to reflect on what had been said, and advise her on what to do. This was the role that Conroy had dreamed of, but Albert occupied it more completely than Conroy ever could have. If the voice was the Queen's voice and the signature was the Queen's signature, the thoughts, and the contents of the letter or document, were Albert's. If their thoughts on almost all topics were the same, it was because she had aligned hers with his to the point where he only had to express a view for it to be also hers – unless her own powerful emotions were engaged. But politics and diplomacy and the ordering of national affairs were only part of Albert's immense range of work. He supervised management of the estates and farms; he was always planning new things for Osborne. From 1852, he had the pleasure of designing and arranging for the building of an entire new castle to replace the unsuitably small house at Balmoral, for in that year they bought the estate. Victoria now had her own Scottish domain.

And then there was the Great Exhibition. It was not, as has sometimes been suggested, Albert's idea. The Society for the Encouragement of Arts, Manufacturers and Commerce and the Society of Arts had held small exhibitions of products during the 1840s, and an energetic figure, Henry Cole, a senior civil servant and a dynamic doer in the best Utilitarian tradition, conceived the idea of a much larger exhibition, of all trades and all nations. Cole fired the Prince with enthusiasm for it, not a difficult task, and Albert took it up with zeal. He headed the commission of distinguished individuals who planned the exhibition and brought it to fruition in little more than a year. Good fortune, at the eleventh hour, brought them the brilliant design of Joseph Paxton for an exhibition hall – a vast prefabricated building of steel and glass that could be put up in Hyde Park and then dismantled. Like every other large-scale new idea in English life, it attracted fierce and vocal criticism as a waste of money, a futile effort to which no one would come, and an ostentatious temple to Mammon, confirming the increasing godlessness and materialism of the times. In Parliament, in the press, the scheme was condemned by its opponents, who included most of those who disliked modernism or Free Trade. As the Prince was acknowledged as its figurehead, he shared in the obloquy. If it was a folly, it would be Albert's folly. If it was a disaster, it would be Albert's disaster. Unweariedly, he laboured, persuaded, wrote voluminously, offered suggestions, drew plans, and kept his committee together. And when it opened, on time, on 1 May 1851, as the Queen ecstatically recorded, it was Albert's triumph.

> 'The glimpse of the transepts through the iron gates, the waving palms, flowers, statues, myriads of people filling the galleries and seats around, with the flourish of trumpets as we entered, gave us a sensation which I shall never forget and I felt much moved ... . The sight as we came to the middle where the steps and a chair (which I did *not* sit on) were placed, with the beautiful crystal fountain just in front of it, was magical – so vast, so glorious, so touching, One felt – as so many did whom I have since spoken to – filled with devotion, more so than by any service which I have ever heard, The tremendous cheers, the joy expressed in every face, the immensity of the building, the mixture of palms, flowers, trees, statues, fountains, the organ (with 400 instruments and 500 voices; which sounded like nothing) and my beloved husband, the author of this 'peace Festival' which united the industry of all the nations of the earth – all this was moving indeed, and it was and is a day to live forever.'

As Queen she would have formally opened the Exhibition in any case; but to open this unique event, so much the creation of Albert, was a special delectation. In her diary she picked on what no doubt had always been high in Albert's mind, the 'peace' aspect of the show. It was not just a trade event, not just a monument to an amazing fifty years of invention and industrial productivity. He saw it, like Free Trade, as a symbol of a world where peace would replace war, where nations would combine in productive and profitable exchange of commodities and goods. More than six million entry tickets were sold, and visitors did indeed come from round the globe to see it. The voices of the cavillers were drowned by the tramp of visitors' feet.

The Making of a Mother

Looking back at the Great Exhibition now, one can see aspects of it that were not apparent at the time. Despite the great organ and the invocations of the Archbishop of Canterbury, it was an essentially secular event. Nothing like it had happened before. Cheap railway fares brought a steady flow of visitors from all over the country, to be amazed and impressed by what they saw. Quite unwittingly, the Prince and his colleagues had taken a big step towards a society in which, for most people, religious or religiously based festivals and events would be supplanted by large-scale commercially or state-sponsored events. But it marked one of the highest points of Victoria's long reign: perhaps the highest before her Jubilee, and certainly the happiest and most satisfying for her.

Victoria and Albert were jointly reigning over a kingdom which, though united as a single political entity, was in fact composed of many groups, divided in a variety of ways by social class, sense of nationality, religion, and outlook on life. Many of the divisions cut across one another, sometimes violently. There was plenty of civil disturbance in Victorian Britain, and not only in the new cities and towns. In England, Wales and Scotland, the monarchy was almost universally accepted as a fundamental binding agent within the community, second only to Parliament, or perhaps coming first for some. For many in Ireland this was also true. 'Law and Order' were executed in the Queen's name, but people also looked to the Queen as the trustee of a long-ingrained historic sense of fairness and justice that placed no one above the law. For the great majority of her people she was a remote figure, known only by repute, by newspaper reports, and by rumour and gossip, though postage stamps and the coinage made her chubby profile the best known in the land. Given their devotion to duty, their hard work, and their domestic respectability, Victoria and Albert could not fail to be respected by those who were themselves hardworking, respectable people. Among a smarter and wealthier set, the same characteristics left them open to mockery. The royal couple's desire for seclusion in their own houses was a source of amusement to such people, as if Victoria really did the work of a housewife, or, even more amusingly, Hausfrau, and Albert dug the garden.

The court could still be grand, in fact in some ways grander than it had ever been, but most of the time it did not put on a great display. It was, however, obsessed by protocol, by the need to do things in the proper way; it was decorous, worthy, and dull. Albert and Victoria were not at all interested in 'Society', which in turn pretended to take little interest in them. The English upper classes still produced plenty of loose-living, high-rolling and hard-riding individuals, of the kind who had entertained George IV and Charles II, but Victoria regarded them with scorn and aversion, and was terrified, as her children grew older, that they might fall into this sort of company – and find it congenial. In other circumstances, Victoria might have become more of a society figure, following the eager party-going of her first months as Queen, but it was not Albert's scene. Though he showed them, on one or two occasions, that he could ride to hounds with the best of them, the Prince and the country gentry never took to each other. He was too earnest, too efficient, to have any time for their concept of the gentlemanly life, with its focus on blood sports, dogs and horses.

Closest to the Queen, in terms of attendance on her person and claims on her attention, were the 'three Estates' of Parliament – Lords, Commons and Church. Almost as important were the armed services – Army and Navy. A 'fourth Estate', which she could neither control nor ignore, and which frequently goaded her to fury, was the Press. The aristocracy, the numerically very small upper section of Britain's steep social pyramid, whose Parliamentary power was solidly established in the House of Lords, was of course the closest social group. The royal ladies-in-waiting came from among the wives and sisters of those lords who adhered to the governing party and were of requisite good morals. Ladies-in-waiting took turns, on and off duty at different times of the year. Tedium and inconvenience were often the lot of the ladies, and they did not always relish the task, as would seem from an urgent note from the Queen to the Countess of Gainsborough in November 1850.

> 'Dearest Fanny,
> This is a case of positive necessity, and as *none* of the ladies are forthcoming I fear I must call on you to attend me *to-night*. You did so once in *state* before, and as it is not a *matter* of *pleasure*, but of duty, I am sure you will at once feel you can have no scruple.
> Whenever the Mistress of the Robes does not attend, I *always* have three ladies, as they must take turns in standing behind me.
> Ever yours affectionately, Victoria R.'

The Queen's attitude to the nobility varied according to their individual behaviour and reputations. When she heard about the raffish and sordid private life of Lord Cardigan of Crimea fame, she ordered that her figure should be painted out of a picture which showed the leader of the Light Brigade displaying a scene of Balaclava to a royal party. She could not wholly avoid such people, and royal drawing-room receptions for the aristocracy were an established item in her calendar. Their hostility to Albert fuelled a more general resentment of the nobility, which she also regarded as altogether too luxurious, frivolous, and extravagant, and neglectful of their proper responsibilities to their country and their tenants and retainers. Criticism of others' extravagance might seem to come oddly from a woman who would soon be prepared to spend the colossal sum of £200,000 on a mausoleum for her husband and herself, but Victoria was perfectly capable of closing off her own behaviour and ideas from those of others, and refraining from judgement on herself.

Sometimes it seemed difficult to find enough persons of probity and general suitability to fill all the senior royal household positions. When Lord Derby became Prime Minister in 1852 and sent in a list of proposed changes, Prince Albert, who considered he had assembled 'a very sorry cabinet' (in Victoria's words), wrote him a severe memorandum criticising his proposal to surround the Queen with 'the Dandies of London and the Roués of the Turf'. In a further document, he found it necessary to inform Derby that 'it was a principle of the court not to receive ladies whose characters are under a stigma.' Although, as with Lady Gainsborough, there were a few ladies with whom she could unbend sufficiently to use their first names and use the direct 'I' rather than the formal, impersonal third person, she had no real friend and confidante among her attendants. But she had Albert, her 'all-in-all'.

The Chancellor of the Exchequer and Leader of the House of Commons in Derby's government was Benjamin Disraeli, by now a significant figure in the Conservative Party and a formidable and feared debater. It was one of his duties to write a resumé of daily Parliamentary proceedings for the Queen, something he did with a lightness of touch unusual in such missives. But at this time the Queen did not care for him: she had not forgotten or forgiven his vituperative criticism of Peel, who was now embalmed in her memory as a great statesman who put country before party in a way which none of these more recent politicians could or would emulate. The Commons, as an estate of her realm, was by an immense degree the largest, since it in effect encompassed everyone who was not possessed of an aristocratic title or ordained as a priest of the Church of England. But the commoners within the Queen's sphere of acquaintance and activity were liable to be as rich and influential, and sometimes even as grand, as the earls and viscounts; and often better educated and more dynamic as persons. The English practice of distinguishing between substantive and courtesy titles also put many scions of the aristocracy into the nominal ranks of commoners. Thus Lord Stanley, son of the Earl of Derby, could have himself elected to Parliament and sit in the House of Commons, until his father died and he automatically became a member of the House of Lords and had to vacate his Commons seat. Marriages between the untitled rich and the not-always-rich titled families blurred the vague frontier between these groups. There were large numbers of the new rich anxious to be accepted as part of the 'ruling classes'. It was these kind of commoners, rather than the far more numerous middle class or the even more vastly numerous working class, whom the Queen regularly encountered. She, and Prince Albert even more so, liked them (so long as they were respectable, and usually they were more sober and sedate than the old aristocracy) because they were the people who got things done.

Florence Nightingale was a good example, though unusual because of her sex. In January 1856, the Queen had written to her, at her hospital in the Crimea.

> 'I need hardly repeat to you how warm my admiration is for your services, which are fully equal to those of my dear and brave soldiers, whose sufferings you have had the *privilege* of alleviating in so merciful a manner.'

She expressed the hope that they would meet on Miss Nightingale's return, and enclosed a brooch, 'which, I hope you will wear as a mark of the high approbation of your Sovereign!' They did meet, on numerous occasions. Florence Nightingale was no more easily overawed than the Queen herself and Victoria, one suspects, was just a little in awe of one who had vanquished her generals and dismissed them as 'fossils'.

The only genuinely working-class people whom the Queen was liable to encounter were her own servants. Domestic servants, particularly those employed by royalty, formed a very distinct section of the 'lower classes', being carefully selected and trained to deference and discretion. But the Queen regarded her personal maid, Annie Macdonald – significantly a Highland woman – as a friend, recording the death of her 'good, faithful maid' in 1897 as a missed friend along with Princess Mary of Cambridge. In 1865 she commented that 'I would as soon clasp the poorest widow in the land to my heart as I would a Queen or any other in high position.' By that time, of course, she was a widow herself, steeped in self-pity. To some degree her attitude was influenced by an exalted form of noblesse oblige: conscious of how her rank separated her from everyone, she tried to remember the essential humanity she shared with all her subjects, and to behave accordingly, since one can never be 'sufficiently loving, kind, and considerate to those beneath one.' She found such maxims easiest to practise during her Balmoral sojourns in which she would visit and talk to the cottagers on the estate. Otherwise her acquaintance with the mass of her subjects was inevitably confined to driving past them as they stood in ranks on the pavements to watch her go by. On such occasions, as on her Dublin visit, she looked as sharply at them as they did at her. Though always distrustful of the potential of a large mass of people to form a revolutionary mob, Victoria did not form part of the large section of the upper classes who opposed political reform. When Disraeli took his great step in 1867 to 'dish the Whigs' by extending voting rights to a million householders, she was thoroughly in favour. Her instinct concurred with Albert's teaching and Disraeli's belief, that by encouragement and emancipation of the 'respectable classes' the security of the monarchy would be increased rather than diminished.

The Church of England formed a small but highly significant 'Estate of the realm'. It was in certain ways a department of state, with the Queen as its supreme governor. All its bishops sat by right in the House of Lords, as the Lords Spiritual. They were appointed by the Queen, on the advice of the Prime Minister. The Church was extremely wealthy, supported not only by its own large landholdings and endowments, but also by tithes which by law were levied on all its parishioners, whether or not they were members or even adherents. It was seamlessly attached to the country's monarchic constitution; the coronation was a religious ceremony and the Queen reigned, as the inscription on every penny reminded, Dei Gratia, by the grace of God. Victoria was a sincere believer in Christianity but her relations with the Church of which she was head were not always harmonious. Her unwavering faith in the Holy Trinity was often expressed in a confused manner. At her coronation she had solemnly sworn to uphold 'the Protestant Religion' and regarded this for the rest of her life as a sacred duty. But she found that the Anglican Church contained several different and conflicting views on how Protestantism should be expressed and practised. The divisions were not clear-cut. In terms of practice, there was a range from the 'Low Church' clerics whose views were close to Lutheranism and even Calvinism to the 'High Church' element which laid great emphasis on the continuing Catholicism of the Church and consequently on the importance of ritual, traditional observance, and ceremoniousness. In terms of expression, there were clergymen at all levels between high and low who believed that the Church should become more spiritual, or more involved with the new and much more fluid urban society which England was becoming. Evangelical pressure groups at the low end wanted to root out the Anglo-Catholic tendency which was at its strongest mid-century. The Anglo-Catholics pressed their own views with vigour.

A further group, regarded with horror by both these sides, used modern scholarship and a scientific approach to question the reliability of the Old Testament as history: Bishop Colenso of Natal was tried for heresy on this account. Prince Albert had been sympathetic to him, and the Princess Royal maintained this support, while the Queen herself, after Albert's death, agreed with Vicky that what she had heard made her feel 'just as you and dear Papa would'. Intellectual and spiritual fervour was apparent on both sides. In the middle of this, there was a group known as the 'Broad Church' which in essence sought to appreciate and preserve the capacity of the Church of England to hold a variety of points of view within its own tenets and forms. The more extreme thinkers on each side regarded the Broad Church with contempt. Though the controversy gripped the Church for several decades, it rarely aroused a wider interest. The Church of England seemed to be focused on its own internal struggle while Methodists, Baptists, and other

Non-conformists were more engaged with the needs of the times. But all churches were struggling against an increasingly secular and material-minded tide of thought.

The Queen's own Church predilections were undoubtedly 'Low', but more than that, they scarcely conformed with some of the basic beliefs of that form of Protestantism which she had sworn, and indeed sincerely strove, to defend. The ideas of hell and damnation were repugnant to her; and Princess Louise once told a Scots minister that her mother did not altogether believe in the devil. She made little secret of the fact that she preferred the more austere and avowedly Calvinist form of worship of her other Established Church, the Church of Scotland, to that of the English Church. She was intensely hostile to the 'Puseyites' or 'Tractarians', named after Dr Edward Pusey of Oxford University, who had begun writing his Tracts for the Times in 1834, before she had acceded to the throne, and made little attempt to distinguish between the Anglo-Catholicism he expounded, and the Roman Catholicism to which some of his associates, like John Henry Newman and Henry Manning, eventually 'defected'. In 1852, Albert noted in one of his many memoranda that in a discussion between Lord Derby, as new Prime Minister, himself, and the Queen, Victoria had 'expressed to him her sense of the importance not to have Puseyites or Romanisers recommended for appointments in the Church as bishops or clergymen.' In 1850, when the Pope established a set of Roman Catholic dioceses in England for the first time since the Reformation, there was a political storm. Lord John Russell's government passed legislation to make this 'papal aggression' illegal. Victoria was in a quandary. She was outraged by what she saw as an act of presumption, but she was also keenly aware that she was Queen of several million Catholics, and that in recent years the Irish influx had greatly increased the number of Roman Catholics in England. She deplored the wild excesses of anti-Catholic feeling that were being displayed, writing to Russell that ...

> '... the Queen deeply regrets the abuse of the Roman
> Catholic religion which takes place at all these meetings,
> etc. She thinks it unchristian and unwise, and trusts
> that it will soon cease ... .'

Victoria favoured the Broad Church and her natural desire was to promote its adherents to deaneries and bishoprics, a policy not designed to appeal to the Evangelical or Anglo-Catholic wings. As she insisted on her right to veto, if not to appoint, her advisers often had to head her off, pointing out that the much greater numbers, and often the intellectual and spiritual distinction, of others had to be taken into account. Unlike her remote ancestor, King James I and VI, who had said, 'No bishop, no king', she seemed to consider bishops as little more than a necessary evil. 'I don't like bishops,' she told Lady Lytton in 1897, having just entertained a hundred of them at a pan-Anglican convention. When Lady Lytton expressed some shock at this wholesale condemnation, the Queen qualified her sentiment a little, 'I like the man but not the bishop.' Perhaps surprisingly, she was not a Sabbatarian, and the institution of the 'Victorian Sunday' owed nothing to her. She protested vigorously against the dropping of Sunday postal deliveries, proposed in June 1850 by the Christian Tory, Lord Ashley.

> 'The Queen thinks it a very *false* notion of obeying God's
> will, to do what will be the cause of much annoyance and
> possibly of great distress to private families.'

Neither she nor Albert considered that Sundays should be devoted to religious study and contemplation. As one of the founders of Wellington College, a public school set up as a memorial to the first Duke of Wellington, the Prince complained about excessive Chapel attendance, prayers, and Bible study, 'His Royal Highness had the strongest feelings upon the inexpediency of thus making the services of the Church and the study of the Bible irksome to boys.'

The Press was another institution that aroused ambivalent feelings in the Queen. Ever since the days when The Times and other newspapers had opposed the marriage with Albert, she had been uncomfortably aware of the power of a hostile press. She had been impressed by the way in which Palmerston used the Morning Chronicle to promote his own views and justify his own actions during the years when Albert and she had sought to control or remove him. She was always reassured to read nice things about herself; in 1844 when she opened the Royal Exchange in London, she told King Leopold of how well she had been received by the press.

> 'The articles in the papers, too, are most kind and gratifying; they say no Sovereign was more loved than I am (I am bold enough to say), and *that*, from *our happy domestic home* – which gives such a good example. *The Times* you have, and I venture to add a *Chronicle*, as I think it very pretty ... .'

Very often she found the newspapers made less pleasant reading. The Times's hostile attitude to Prussia was particularly vexing to her, especially after Vicky became engaged to Prince Frederick William of Prussia. In 1861, she appealed to Palmerston as the only person who might have any influence with John T Delane, editor of The Times, to get him to moderate his attacks. Palmerston did make an effort, but he pointed out to the Queen that the English newspapers, unlike those in continental countries, were commercial undertakings beyond the control of government or political parties: the Queen knew this perfectly well but also knew that a skilled politician, like Palmerston himself, could manipulate both news and comment. Such a skill, considered as no better than chicanery by Victoria, could not be deployed by the Palace. It was completely alien to her directness and candour.

In May 1849, a fourth attack was made on the Queen, when an Irishman called Hamilton fired a pistol at her while she was out driving with three of the children and her maid, Miss Macdonald. It turned out not to be loaded. 'It did not alarm me at all,' she wrote to Leopold. Hamilton was sentenced to seven years' transportation. In June 1850, as the Queen's carriage was negotiating the entrance to Cambridge House, in Piccadilly, a man sprang from the crowd and struck her violently with his brass-topped walking stick. She was momentarily knocked out. Her assailant, Robert Pate, was seized by furious bystanders; though judged to be of unsound mind, he, too, was sent to a penal colony for seven years. After this, Victoria was understandably more concerned about her safety. 'I own it makes me nervous out driving, and I start at any person coming near the carriage, which I am afraid is natural,' she wrote to Leopold.

Though she did not give up driving in an open carriage, such episodes heightened her appreciation of the seclusion of Osborne, and, even more, Balmoral. The freehold of the Scottish estate was bought for £31,500 in June 1852. Albert had already been designing a building to replace the old house and the foundation stone of the present castle was laid by Victoria on 23 September 1853. By 1855 enough had been constructed for them to begin occupancy. Balmoral Castle was described in Black's Picturesque Tourist of Scotland (1863) as combining ...

> ' ... the more bold and prominent features of the ancient stronghold with the more domestic character of modern civilisation ... the castle, at a distance, looks as if it had been hewn out of one of the huge granite rocks ... all the apartments are characterised by that simplicity of style and purity of taste for which the Royal Family are so remarkable.'

Murray's *Handbook for Scotland* (1894) called the building 'a castellated palatial mansion in the mixed Elizabethan and Scottish style' and commented:

'The interior is not shown [that is, open to the public]; nor, indeed, is there anything within to reward curiosity, the whole arrangement being simple in the extreme, but in perfect good taste, and suited to a Highland residence.'

In style, Balmoral Castle is a wild confusion, but in function, it was very effective. The taste of the interior was not shared by everyone: the profusion of tartan and thistles in carpets, curtains, wallpaper, even linoleum, was felt by many visitors to be overdone; but the Queen was enraptured by the castle's appearance, inside and out, ' ... my dearest Albert's own creation, own work, own building, own laying out ... . The impress of his dear hand has been stamped everywhere.'

Eventually the royal domains on Deeside would reach more than forty thousand acres of woodland and deer forest. One of the places on it the Queen liked best was the little house of Alt-na-Giuthasach, above Loch Muick, where she and Albert sometimes spent a few days. At Balmoral there were usually guests; here they could be as wholly on their own as was possible with the inevitable lady-in-waiting on duty and a team of servants for the catering and housekeeping. Victoria was an accomplished water-colourist and enjoyed sketching and painting the scene, while Albert fished, stalked deer, and kept a close interest in the management of the estate. What Lord Clarendon, the Foreign Secretary, called the 'tartanitis' of the Balmoral household was not confined to interior design. The prince designed a 'Balmoral' tartan and he and his sons adopted the current notion of 'Highland dress' with kilt, great furry sporran, tartan hose and short jacket. The royal enthusiasm for all things Highland (Albert even made some attempt to acquaint himself with Gaelic) undoubtedly helped to popularise and perpetuate the kilt as a uniform for Highland regiments and as an item of Scottish dress. Publication of photographs of the kilted Princes set off a fashion for garbing the boys of well-off families in this way, as far afield as London and even New York. It was one of the very few trends set by the resolutely unfashionable royal family. Access to Balmoral was made much easier by the opening of the Deeside Railway from Aberdeen to Aboyne in 1859; the royal train could now run overnight from Windsor to a station only a few miles from the castle. The advent of the railway also brought the electric telegraph, and a wire was set up from Balmoral to Aboyne. By October 1866, the line was extended to Ballater.

Visits to Balmoral could be rather testing on those for whom exposure to cold fresh air was an unwelcome experience. One of Victoria's qualities was an unusual imperviousness to cold. She detested heat and even as a girl had felt 'poorly and stupefied in hot weather'. In Windsor or Osborne, she was reluctant to have fires and liked to have the windows open. A temperature above 56°F (around 13°C) made her feel uncomfortably warm. But Balmoral was almost 900 feet (282 metres) up in a Scottish glen, and by autumn its chills could be searching. Even the Tsar of Russia, when he visited, felt that Siberia might be warmer. Typically, Victoria never made the slightest concession on this. Because her rooms must be cold, so should those of the rest of the family and of guests. On one occasion, Prince Arthur was made to put out a fire that he had ordered to be lit in his bedroom. Albert suffered from her aversion to warmth, but accepted it for her sake, and frequently wore a fur-lined coat indoors.

The years between 1852 and 1862 were the most contented and fulfilled of Victoria's life. Each year passed in a generally pleasurable routine, intermingled with special events. On the whole she enjoyed carrying out her royal duties, and kept these with a strict formality, not for her own pride but for what she represented (though at a certain level, a degree of personal pride can hardly be excluded). Maturity, marriage, and maternity had increased her confidence. Though small and dumpy ('portly' was her own word) a host of observers testify to her power to dominate a room or assembly. Visiting dignitaries, other than reigning sovereigns, having been presented to her, had to back away from the royal presence, until at a suitable distance they could turn to one side. Those who did not know the etiquette of the court were instructed in how or when to kneel, to bow, and to curtsey. Her inability to make small talk to strangers, especially those she felt ill at ease with, persisted, but in occasions of high formality it could almost seem like part of the necessary procedure. Among the few regular grand occasions she feared and disliked was the State Opening of Parliament, at which, while she sat enthroned and wearing her crown in the House of Lords, the government's legislative programme for the coming Parliamentary session was read out (she always refused to do this) for her by the Lord Chancellor. Her daily attendance to the dispatchers from ministers and colonial governors was greatly eased by Albert, who read them first and prepared short briefings and digests for her and drew her attention to key points.

Of course there were times of trouble and trial. In the latter part of 1853, as hostility grew between the Russian and the Ottoman Empires, Britain was increasingly drawn into the dispute. It was on the advice of the British ambassador at Constantinople that the Turks finally declared war on Russia on 23 October. The Premier, Lord Aberdeen, had been arguing for peace, a policy with which the Queen and Prince agreed, but not all the members of his Conservative-Liberal coalition were in favour. As tension increased, some extraordinary rumours began to circulate in London. Popular opinion was very much against Russia and the Prince's moderation was taken as pro-Russian action 'behind the scenes'. All the latent hostility to the foreign Consort surfaced again. It was said that the government had imprisoned him in the Tower of London; and even that the Queen had been sent there too. Crowds gathered outside it as if an execution were expected. On 16 December further excitement was caused by Lord Palmerston's resignation from the government, in which he had been Home Secretary, ostensibly on the subject of reform. Deeply conservative in domestic matters, he objected to the further measures for electoral reform which his Liberal party colleague, Lord John Russell, was promoting.

By February 1854, the Queen was resigned to the inevitability of war, with Britain and France allied, on Turkey's behalf, against Russia. Once war was declared, her heart was immediately with the soldiers and sailors of her army and navy. 'My whole heart and soul are in the Crimea,' she wrote to King Leopold in November 1854. She proposed a special medal for the troops, promoted Lord Raglan, the commander, to Field Marshal, rejoiced over the victories of Alma and Inkerman, and deplored the heavy loss of life. But in the course of 1855 it became apparent that other enemies – the incompetence of the military staff, and even more, the apparently uncontrollable spread of disease among the troops – were putting the whole expedition in serious danger. Victoria absorbed this unpalatable information with the utmost reluctance, and was most upset when 'poor dear Aberdeen's' unstable coalition finally collapsed, even though its feeble prosecution of the war was its undoing. It soon became clear that the only figure capable of forming a viable coalition government was Palmerston, and the Queen reluctantly commissioned him to do so on 6 February 1855. Whilst it might be hard to see a greater degree of skill in the management of the war, or in the supply of vital resources to the troops, Palmerston's robust style gave confidence to the country and, in the end, to the Queen and Prince as well. Past offences were forgotten; as Prime Minister, Palmerston was much more disposed to keep the Queen informed, and curiously, it was Lord John Russell, who took on the post of Foreign Secretary, who now attracted royal ire for lack of information and consultation.

This was not the first of Britain's wars during Victoria's reign by any means, but it was the first and only one against a European power, whose sovereign she had entertained at Windsor, and to whom she wrote, in diplomatic parlance, as 'My Brother'. To be a reigning queen in time of war is more demanding than to be a king: Victoria had to reflect the national belligerence and also retain a feminine quality of gentleness and sympathy. She achieved it well, not least because she felt both strains of feeling within herself. The novel situation of having France as an ally also brought her into friendly contact with that would-be master of fate and destiny, Napoleon III, the French Emperor, great-nephew of Britain's great enemy Napoleon Bonaparte, who paid a state visit to Britain (where he had once been, and would be again, a political refugee) in April 1855. Though she had regarded him as an adventurer, he quickly won her interest and admiration; she noted his 'power of fascination, the effect of which upon all those who become more intimately acquainted with him is most sensibly felt. How far he is actuated by a strong moral sense of right and wrong is difficult to say.' Victoria made a reciprocal visit in August, to a Paris which was put en fête for her, and which she greatly enjoyed and appreciated, calling her stay 'the pleasantest and most interesting and triumphant ten days that I think I ever passed.'

Prince Albert was, as the Queen observed, less taken with the new closeness to France than she was. His interest had always been focused on Germany and his ambition remained to see the patchwork of German kingdoms, principalities, and duchies welded into unity under the leadership of Prussia, which he always assumed to be the most politically developed and socially enlightened of the German states. It was in Victoria's reign that the notion of a British-French entente cordiale was first uttered, long before 1904, but Albert would have preferred an axis of cordial understanding between London and Berlin – this, he believed, would drive forward both peace and prosperity in Europe. Both he and the Queen were very pleased when the twenty-four-year-old Frederick William, eldest son of the Crown Prince of Prussia, expressed a wish to marry Vicky, the Princess Royal, during a visit to Balmoral in September 1855. The Queen saw it, as she reported to King Leopold, as his wish 'to belong to our Family'. She appears not to have considered it was rather more of a wish to import her daughter into the Hohenzollern family. Vicky was only fifteen, and it was considered desirable that 'Fritz' should not formally propose until the following year. And the intention was to keep the matter secret until then. It proved impossible to do this, and to the distress and irritation of the parents, the story was soon out, and the engagement was attacked in some quarters in both England and Prussia even before it was formalised. The Times described the Hohenzollerns as a 'paltry dynasty'. But the plans went ahead and the wedding was celebrated at the Chapel Royal in St James's Palace in January 1858. There had been controversy over this – Prussian tradition demanded that the Crown Prince be married in Prussia, but Queen Victoria was not having that. The Foreign Secretary was instructed to inform the Prussian ambassador:

> 'Whatever may be the usual practice of Prussian princes, it is not *every* day that one marries the eldest daughter of the Queen of England. The question must therefore be considered as settled and closed.'

With Vicky's marriage, the first of the children departed from home, aged only seventeen. Although eight children remained in the household – the youngest, Beatrice, being less than a year old – Victoria found it extremely difficult to accept that her daughter was a married woman with a household of her own. She demanded letters on a daily basis and herself poured out a torrent of advice and directives. Stockmar, still acting as the conscience of the royal family, and in everybody's confidence, pressed Albert to lean on the Queen to reduce the frequency and moderate the tone, of her letters to Vicky. The Prussian court had a protocol of its own, in many ways more old-style, formal, and ceremonious than that of Britain, but in Victoria's view, Vicky was still Princess Royal of England and should abide by English royal custom in every way from the arrangements of royal mourning to the installation of flush toilets. But though Albert tried to restrain his wife, he, too, bore responsibility for Vicky's difficulties, having instilled into his daughter the sense that she had a mission to change things in her new country. Implicit in all this was his desire to see Prussia become the Britain of Germany, with a constitutional monarchy and no more ceremonial flummery than was necessary to underline the status of the monarchy. The demands of both her parents did not make Vicky's life any easier. Like her mother, she conceived very soon after marriage and again Victoria tried to take control. An English nursery, with English nanny, was established in preparation. But there was a much more serious issue. The Princess was sure there was something amiss with her pregnancy, though the Prussian doctors dismissed her fears. Only when labour began was it clear that the baby was in the dangerous breech position. Queen Victoria had sent two doctors, Sir James Clark and Dr E Martin, and her own midwife, Mrs Innocent, with a supply of chloroform. It was Martin who saved both mother and baby during an intensely painful and difficult birth, but even so, the baby's left shoulder had been dislocated, and his left arm never developed properly. Thus the Queen's first grandchild, the future Kaiser Wilhelm II, came into the world.

Victoria, in giving birth to Beatrice at the comparatively advanced age, especially for that era, of 38, had availed herself of chloroform as an anaesthetic for the second time, having been first given it on the birth of Leopold in 1853, when it was still a very new drug. She was given enough to make her drowsy but not unconscious, and welcomed it without reservation. When news of her dosing came out, there was some controversy, but her pioneering example encouraged many obstetricians and expectant mothers to do the same. Despite her long-held objections to the physical demands of motherhood, she expressed a yearning to have a tenth child. The question of how far she and Albert practised any of the forms of birth control then available is obscure, but she is said, when Sir James Clark advised her to have no more pregnancies after Beatrice, to have asked him, 'Can I have no more fun in bed?'

The Crimean War had ended in March 1856 and Victoria was both pleased and relieved by the terms of the peace treaty. She made Palmerston a Knight of the Garter. In addition to the

Crimean service medal (given to all who served in the war, with the Queen – for the first time in British history – personally handing it to a select number of ordinary troops as well as to all the officers), one of the results of the war was the institution of a special award for extreme bravery, the Victoria Cross. The idea was introduced in 1855 and the Queen of course took a very close interest, supervising the design and herself choosing the simple motto, 'For Valour'. She also considered that holders should bear 'some distinctive mark after their name', but feeling that VC would not do, because it signified 'Vice-Chancellor', she opted for BVC, 'bearer of the Victoria Cross'.

Influenced both by Albert's undoubtedly valuable contributions to the planning and waging of the war, and by her re-established friendship with Palmerston, who for his part handsomely acknowledged the virtues and important role of Albert, the Queen resumed her old quest to have her husband given official status in his own right. She had abandoned her thought of 'King' Albert, but in May 1856 she drew up a memorandum on the subject.

> ' ... after considering the question for nearly *sixteen years*, I have come to the conclusion that the title which is now by universal consent given him of 'Prince Consort', with the highest rank in and out of Parliament after the Queen, and before every other Prince of the Royal Family, should be the one assigned to husband of the Queen regnant *once and for all.*'

One of the things that troubled her was the thought that Albert's sons, as they grew up, would take official precedence over their father, something she considered intolerable. She hoped for an Act of Parliament to confirm this, but in the end, on the advice of Lord Derby, the matter was not put before Parliament and instead the Prince Consort's status was formally confirmed by royal Letters Patent published on 25 June 1857, specifically for Prince Albert.

Bertie, the Prince of Wales, was then sixteen. At eighteen he would become of age and entitled to claim his proper precedence on state occasions, so Albert's superior dignity was established none too soon. Bertie remained a focus of parental concern and anxiety. Despite the attentions of numerous tutors, he remained uninterested, indeed ever more determinedly uninterested, in the kind of intellectual pursuits in which his father and elder sister revelled. He had been sent on a carefully supervised version of the European 'grand tour', without gaining the sort of cultural insights that Albert had found on his own visit to Italy with Stockmar, long ago. At seventeen, he was presented with a document from both his parents that prompted him to burst into tears. In Strachey's description, it was a direction ' henceforward to perform the duties of a Christian gentleman.' The memorandum said:

'Life is composed of duties, and in the due, punctual, and cheerful performance of them the true Christian, true soldier, and true gentleman is recognised .... A new sphere of life will open for you in which you will have to be taught what to do and what not to do, a subject requiring study more important than any in which you have hitherto been engaged.'

The existence of 'Society', of the swells, the gamblers, the racing men and racy women, of days of delicious leisure, of long uproarious dinners at which, quite contrary to the practice insisted on by his mother, the men sat long over their port and smoked large cigars, could not be concealed from Bertie, and he felt unspeakable yearnings towards it. As if they detected this urge – and perhaps they did – his parents also drew up a lengthy document intended for the guidance of those gentlemen who were selected to attend upon the Prince of Wales, and laying weight upon the responsibility of their position and the trust placed in their 'flattering selection' as guides and mentors to the young Prince. At eighteen, Bertie was sent to Oxford for a time, living in seclusion with his selected gentlemen but nevertheless making a few undesirable friendships with some aristocratic young bloods. He was then moved to Cambridge, where his father was Chancellor. At nineteen, for the first time, he undertook a substantial duty on his own, with the Duke of Newcastle as his principal attendant, making an official visit to Canada and the United States, where he was received in Washington by President Buchanan. There were political risks here, as relations between the United States and Great Britain were traditionally fraught and edgy, but the North American visit was a great success. Given a chance, Bertie was affable and good-natured, and had a gift for easy conversation which his parents notably lacked. Victoria was delighted, and warm in her praise, 'all the more as he was never spared any reproof', but Albert's reaction was curmudgeonly, giving Bertie no credit but putting down the warmth of his reception to the fact that he was his mother's son.

From the first news of the outbreak of the Indian 'Mutiny' in the summer of 1857, the attention of Victoria and Albert was seized by events in the subcontinent. The armed forces were being reduced, following the Crimean War, and the Queen's thoughts, as ever, were first for her soldiers, and for effective supply to the suddenly overstretched British regiments. Disraeli was among the first to realise that no mere mutiny but something more like a national revolt was taking place. In an unusual piece of understatement, the Queen wrote to Palmerston that 'this hardly appears the moment to make savings in the Army estimates.' Though shocked and appalled by the reports of atrocities committed upon British women and children, the Queen, who had the benefit of sane and balanced reports from the Governor-General, Lord Canning, did not give way to a spirit of indiscriminate revenge. Canning advised her:

> 'There is a rabid and indiscriminate vindictiveness abroad, even amongst many who ought to set a better example, which it is impossible to contemplate without something like a feeling of shame for one's fellow-countrymen.'

He was contemptuously denounced by those who committed, encouraged, and condoned British atrocities as 'Clemency' Canning, but he had the Queen as a staunch supporter. She did not share the racial prejudices of many of the India-based British, and in as far as the Indian population could be said to be her subjects, she felt it her responsibility and duty to be their Queen as much as she was of her British subjects. In 1858, that duty became more of a reality when the British Parliament assumed the government of India from the old East India Company, and Governor-General Canning became her first Viceroy of India. Disraeli, reporting to her as Leader of the Commons, wrote of the measure:

> 'It is only the ante-chamber of an imperial palace; and your Majesty would do well to deign to consider the steps which are now necessary to influence the opinions and affect the imaginations of the Indian population.'

She took a very close interest in the new government of India, insisting to Derby that a proclamation of the principles of Indian government should be redrafted ...

> ' ... bearing in mind that it is a female Sovereign who speaks to more than a hundred millions of eastern people on assuming the direct government over them ... . Such a document should breathe feelings of generosity, benevolence, and religious toleration.'

In this, not for the first or last time, Victoria's rhetoric went some way past reality. It was not she who was assuming the direct government over the millions. But she and Albert never forgot an old precept Stockmar had taught them, that royal power was constantly under threat of curtailment: 'No opportunity should be let slip of vindicating the legitimate position of the Crown.' Her letters to Prime Ministers, especially those whom, like Derby, she did not quite trust, often exaggerated her own role, in line with another Stockmarian dictum, that she should regard herself as a sort of perpetual head of government, with Prime Ministers, as heads of political parties, there to see that Parliament carried out her wishes. Such a notion was alien to more than a hundred and thirty years of Parliamentary government and practice, but the constitutional position was sufficiently vague for it to be at least a debating point. The old Baron's visits had, however, become rarer, and Victoria had gently chided him for not replying to letters: he was 'naughty Stockmar'. He last came to England in the year of the Princess Royal's marriage. Now seventy, he retired to his home in Coburg in provincial Germany, far from the great capitals where he had been a familiar and portentous figure for so long, but he continued to write and receive letters, with Prince Albert among his correspondents.

In September 1860, the sense of freedom which the Queen always felt at Balmoral took a new form, when she and Albert made a brief but 'most delightful incognito expedition' across the hills to stay a night at the inn at Grantown-on-Spey, travelling under assumed names. She and Albert were 'Lord and Lady Churchill'; the actual Lady Churchill, who was of the party, went as Miss Spencer; General Grey assumed the style of Dr Grey. Two maids had been sent ahead, and the only other servants were 'our two excellent Highlanders, viz. Albert's first stalker or head keeper, and my own Highland servant and factotum – both excellent, intelligent, devoted people.' Only when the party had left the inn was the incognito revealed, and the Queen was delighted by the inhabitants' reported surprise. The pleasure she had in the 'if only they knew' feeling was exceeded only by her relish of their discovery of Whom their visitor had really been. They returned to Balmoral, partly by a hired carriage 'with a pair of wretched tired horses', partly by pony, and finally in their own carriage.

On 15 March 1861, the Queen, in London, received an urgent message from Sir James Clark. The Duchess of Kent was dying. She hurried to her mother's house at Frogmore on the Windsor estate. The seventy-four-year-old Duchess had been diagnosed two years earlier – unknown to the Queen, since Albert had not told her – as suffering from an incurable tumour. Victoria spent the night at Frogmore, and was at her mother's side when she died around nine o'clock on the following morning. Her half-brother Charles, Prince of Leiningen, had died in November 1856, but he had not been especially close to her. Most people of her age had more experience of death, and of witnessing death, than Victoria had. Being in her mother's house, among her mother's possessions, brought back poignant memories of earlier times. For a time her feelings almost overcame her. Since her marriage, her relationship with her mother had been far better and happier, but the period of estrangement bore heavily on her. Her mother's ambitions and schemes were forgotten, among all the evidence of how much she had loved and doted on her daughter: the souvenirs and relics of Victoria's childhood years, carefully preserved, were there to prove it. The Queen felt an 'immeasurable' sense of loss. She wrote to King Leopold on 26 March:

> 'The constant intercourse of *forty-one* years cannot cease without the total want of power of *real enjoyment* of *anything*. A sort of cloud which hangs over you, and seems to *oppress* everything – and a positive weakness in the powers of reflection and mental exertion. The doctors *tell* me I *must not* attempt to *force* this. Long conversation, loud talking, the talking of many people together, I can't bear yet.'

Once in her diary she had written, 'I don't believe Ma ever really loved me.' If she remembered having such thoughts, it only increased her sense of bereavement and lost opportunities. Her sense of personal isolation was heightened. In the same letter to Leopold, she wrote:

> 'Except Albert (whom I very often don't see but very little in the day) I have no *human* being except

our children, and that is not the same *Verhältniss* [relationship] to *open* oneself to; and besides, a *woman* requires woman's society and sympathy sometimes, as men do *men's*.

Though she told him that there was general approval of the manner in which she had shown her grief, to most observers, her reaction seemed overwrought. It was rumoured that she had broken down mentally.

By late May, she was again attending to official business, and in August made her second visit to Ireland, a more subdued affair than the first. During the Cambridge long vacation, Bertie was attached to the Grenadier Guards regiment, as part of his training regime, and went with them on exercises at the Curragh Camp, outside Dublin. The Queen watched a parade there, in which he marched past with his company, and she felt he 'did not look at all so very small'. After a westward excursion to see the beauties of Killarney, the royal party moved on to the bracing airs of Balmoral.

Here the Queen's spirits began to revive. Two more incognito expeditions were made, this time enlarged by Princess Alice and her fiancé, Prince Louis of Hesse-Darmstadt. On 21 October, she wrote to Leopold:

'We have had a most beautiful week … . I going out every day about twelve or half past, taking luncheon with us, carried in a basket on the back of a Highlander, and served by an *invaluable* Highland servant I have, who is *my factotum here*, and takes the most wonderful care of me, combining the offices of groom, footman, page, and *maid*, I might almost say, as he is *so* handy about cloaks and shawls, etc. He always leads my pony, and always attends me out of doors, and *such* a good, handy, *faithful*, attached servant I have nowhere; it is quite a sorrow for me to leave him behind.'

Albert, whose health had not been good throughout 1860 and 1861, who had borne, with Alice, the brunt of supporting the Queen's distress at her mother's death, and who worked so hard that Victoria complained of hardly seeing him, also found the stay at Balmoral to be a tonic.

The return to Windsor, always bemoaned by the Queen, this year was especially trying. Albert and she were worried about events in Prussia, where Vicky's father-in-law, now King William III, was intent on setting up an authoritarian royal dictatorship far removed from Albert's dream of a Liberal beacon-state. The Queen fretted about anti-Prussianism in the British press. Their Coburg cousins, the King of Portugal, and his brother, had both died of typhoid fever. The American Civil War had broken out and Britain, though officially neutral, was suspected by the Union government of having undue sympathy for the Confederates. Such events were beyond their control and one of Albert's favourite pieces of advice to his wife was to 'take things as God sends them', but both of them were profoundly shocked by something far less momentous, but much closer to home and seeming to shatter their own cherished plans. While in Ireland, Bertie had disgraced himself.

For the three months of his attachment to the Grenadiers, Prince Albert had spelled out, in the usual way, what the Prince of Wales should achieve. Not only was he to master the duties of every grade from Ensign up, but he was also expected to be able to command a battalion and manoeuvre a brigade in field operations. It was an absurd notion even if the Prince had shown any aptitude, like his younger brother Arthur, for the military life, but Albert, at the Curragh parade, had been disappointed to see his son trusted to command only a company. As at Cambridge, Bertie was housed with his 'gentlemen' at some distance from the officers' mess where the other junior officers were. But on the last night of the exercises, there was a ball given at the Mansion House in Dublin, with the Prince as guest of honour. When he returned to his own quarters, he found that a lively and attractive young 'actress', Nellie Clifden, well known to the other officers, had somehow been smuggled in. At least, that is how the event has been treated. Whether or not he was a party to it, the Prince happily took the opportunity to become what one of his biographers referred to as 'introduced to dissipation'. No more might have come of what was a lighthearted episode, but it was too good a story to be kept quiet, and rumours about the Prince of Wales and the actress began to spread. Someone wrote with the story to Stockmar in Coburg, and the Baron, inevitably, all his natural concern and officiousness aroused, wrote to the Prince Consort. Albert received the news on 12 November, by which time Bertie was back at Cambridge. Disbelieving at first, he made enquiries and found that the gossip was based on fact. Twenty years of careful nurturing and stringent moral education lay in ruins. The paternal horror was almost as hysterical as the maternal grief of earlier in the year. Himself a model of sexual rectitude, Albert clearly felt a profound sense of personal disgust, quite apart from his firm belief that the monarchy's survival was dependent on its being, and being known to be, morally beyond reproach.

The weather that November reflected the Prince's feelings – cold, wet, and miserable. On 22 November, he visited the new army staff college building at Sandhurst and was thoroughly soaked. On 25 November, he went with Victoria on one of her pilgrimages to her mother's mausoleum at Frogmore and returned feeling thoroughly unwell. Nevertheless, next day he went to Cambridge for a face-to-face meeting with his errant son. Bertie was contrite and humble, and the visit ended in reconciliation. No more would be said. But after his return, the Prince Consort felt ill and exhausted, 'at a low ebb'. Still, there was duty to be attended to. A serious diplomatic crisis with Abraham Lincoln's government in Washington was brewing. A Union warship had stopped a British vessel, RMS Trent, on the high seas and taken off two Confederate envoys bound for Europe. This was considered a gross outrage and violation of international law by the nation that claimed to rule the waves. Lord Russell, as Foreign Minister, had composed a despatch to

Washington which was, in effect, an ultimatum. War with the American North seemed entirely possible. The despatch was submitted to the Queen in draft, and though, as she recalled later, he could hardly hold his pen, Albert read it and was alarmed by its phrasing, which demanded a humiliating climb-down by the American government and allowed it no way to retreat gracefully from a grave diplomatic embarrassment. He suggested a form of toning-down, which would allow Washington to express regret in a mutually acceptable way, and this was incorporated in the final message. The RMS Trent incident ended without causing transatlantic warfare. It was Albert's last service to the government of Great Britain. His illness grew worse, and he was unable to leave his bed.

His doctor was Sir James Clark, in whom the Queen was almost alone in having faith; Palmerston, having visited the Prince on 1 December, urged her to consult another doctor, but she did not do so, assuring him that Albert had no more than a 'feverish cold'. By 7 December it was clear that the Prince had typhoid, and other eminent doctors were now brought in, including William Jenner, a specialist in typhoid. The Queen was still expressing optimism about his recovery, encouraged by Clark. Albert himself knew better. When Alice told him she had written to Vicky to report that he was seriously ill, he said, 'You did wrong. You should have told her I am dying.' On 9 December, the Queen wrote, with a sad unintentional irony, to her uncle that 'Every day ... is bringing us nearer the end of this tiresome illness.' On 12 December, she again reported favourably, but by 13 December it was clear that the Prince's condition was critical. Alice telegraphed for Bertie to come urgently, and he arrived at three o'clock the following morning. That day the Prince was only semiconscious; as he weakened, pneumonia was setting in and his breathing grew terribly laboured. The Queen now knew she was sitting by a deathbed, and the younger children were brought in to say a last goodbye, though Albert was unaware of them being there. At six o'clock her despair was too great to allow her to remain in the room, but she rallied herself, and returned, to bend over the dying man and whisper, *'Es ist kleines Fräuchen'* [It's little wifey], his own private term of endearment for her. Watching and waiting with her were Bertie, Alice, and Lenchen. She did not see the moment of death, which happened at about a quarter to eleven – whether by chance or intention, she left the room to use an adjacent lavatory. When she came in again, she saw at once that he was dead.

'Oh, this is death, I know it. I have seen it before,' she exclaimed. She kissed his forehead and cried out, 'Oh! My dear darling.' For a few moments she went on calling out endearments to him, holding his already cold hand, then sank to her knees, unable to speak or weep.

Bertie helped her into the next room. Albert had told him that his mother did not know of the Curragh escapade, but in fact she did know. As he held her in his arms, he promised to do everything he could to help her. 'I am sure, my dear boy, you will,' she answered. Seeming calm, but shocked, she spoke to the doctors and the members of the household who had also been there. With the Duchess of Atholl, she went back again into the room where Albert lay, and her composure gave way. She threw herself on the bed, her arms outstretched over her husband's body.

'Oh, Duchess! He is dead! He is dead!' she cried.

CHAPTER 4

The Making of a Widow

Prince Albert's death, for which she was completely unprepared, was the pivotal event of Queen Victoria's life, and brought to her her worst moments. In almost every aspect of her life she had come to depend on him. The stiff, reserved, sensitive young German, chosen to be husband for the British Queen at least as much by destiny as by his own volition, had come to be the supreme and all-embracing influence in her life, 'my all-in-all'. Not only that, he had made for himself a position of importance, trust, and respect within the British system of constitutional government. Senior politicians and courtiers did not underestimate his role, though it was inevitably less clear to people who were not at the centre of affairs. They now looked to the future with some trepidation. Lord Clarendon wrote of Albert's death as 'a national calamity of far greater importance than the public dream of.' Disraeli wrote more emotionally:

> 'With Prince Albert we have buried our sovereign. This German prince has governed England for twenty-one years with a wisdom and energy such as none of our kings have ever shown ... .'

Victoria felt herself utterly bereft. On 20 December, she wrote to King Leopold:

> 'MY OWN DEAREST, KINDEST *FATHER*, – For as such have I ever loved you! The poor fatherless baby of eight months is now the utterly broken-hearted and crushed widow of forty-two! My *life* as a *happy* one is ended! The world is gone for me! If I *must* live on (and I will do nothing to make me worse than I am), it is henceforth for our poor fatherless children – for my

unhappy country, which has lost *all* in losing him – and in *only* doing what I know and *feel* he would wish, for he is near me – his spirit will guide and inspire! But oh! To be cut off in the prime of life – to see our pure, happy, quiet, domestic life, which *alone* enabled me to bear my *much* disliked position, CUT OFF at forty-two – when I *had* hoped with such instinctive certainty that God never *would* part us, and would let us grow old together (though *he* always talked of the shortness of life) is too *awful*, too cruel … . His purity was too great, his aspiration *too high*, for this poor *miserable* world! His great soul is *now only* enjoying *that* of which it was worthy!'

Though often scarcely able to speak at this time, articulacy with the pen had not deserted her, and this letter sums up much of her powerful and conflicting feelings in that dark December. The shock of the blow – the sense of emptiness – the belief that the rest of the world could not understand what it, and she, had lost – the sense that he was still somehow near her – the awareness of the burdens she would now have to bear alone – these were the things uppermost in her mind as she sank into grief. Her religious faith survived, and was sharpened by, her loss. Albert had believed in a future life and in their reunion in that life; and she clung to that that thought even as she felt that God had dealt her a heavy – and unfair – stroke. What had she done to deserve this pain, why did she now have to confront a blank, bleak yet demanding future? She felt this strongly but did not explore it in her own thoughts; it was rather that Albert was too good, his soul too beautiful, for this world. And yet there was an element of dramatisation and self-regard in it, a middle-aged mother of nine, contemplating herself as a 'fatherless baby of eight months' as she indeed had been but was scarcely likely to remember.

Perhaps only one other person was as deeply affected, and similarly felt the Prince Consort's death as a grievous personal blow. That was Baron Stockmar. Despite a lifetime of activity in European diplomacy, he saw Albert's career as his principal life's work, a triumphant vindication of his ideals, his tuition, and his counselling. Now he said he had nothing left to live for, and would soon follow Albert. He died in 1863, aged seventy-six.

Queen Victoria still had much to live for. She had young children; she had grandchildren. There was her 'much disliked' position – she had duties and responsibilities that could not be shaken off. And unlike her husband, she had a powerful will to live. Albert had sensed this. Sir Theodore Martin's biography of the Prince noted how once he had told her, in the German which they customarily used for private or intimate conversation, 'I do not cling to life; you do, but I set no store by it. I am sure, if I had a severe illness, I should give up at once, I should not struggle for life. I have no tenacity of life.' Such willingness to slip away might have angered his widow, but there is no trace of that; nor did she blame the doctor she had selected for him, though Clarendon confided to the Duchess of Manchester, Mistress of the Robes, that 'it is horrible to think that such a life may have been sacrificed to Sir James Clark's selfish jealousy of every member of his profession.'

Palmerston, her Prime Minister, was not among those who encouraged the Queen to mourn unduly. By 29 December, he was writing to …

> ' … humbly express a hope that the intensity of your Majesty's grief may not lead your Majesty to neglect your health, the preservation of which is so important for the welfare of your Majesty's children, and for that of your Majesty's devotedly attached and affectionate subjects; and which is so essentially necessary to enable your Majesty to perform those duties which it will be the object of your Majesty's life to fulfil.'

This was intended as a clear reminder of royal duty: six reiterations of 'your Majesty' in one sentence were to remind her of who, and what, she was. It was of no avail. A subtler politician would have waited longer and used a less bluff approach. The stricken Queen did not appreciate being told to pull herself together in the name of a duty which she saw as an almost intolerable burden. In any case, she was quite incapable of doing so. Her nurse and mainstay at this time was the eighteen-year-old Princess Alice, who looked after her with single-minded care. It was Alice who saw government ministers and brought their papers to the Queen, who gave her draughts of laudanum to help her sleep, who held her in her fits of anguish, who saw to it that the normalities of domestic life at Windsor and Osborne went on. Another source of consolation the Queen drew on was her youngest child, Princess Beatrice (Benjamina to the family), who in the mornings came and climbed into her bed, to be passionately, despairingly hugged. Among the sharpest pangs the new widow suffered were those felt in the marital bed, where no more caresses, murmured German endearments, and 'fun' were to be had. 'I am, alas, not old,' she wrote, 'and my feelings are strong and warm; my love is ardent.'

When a meeting of the Privy Council became necessary, the counsellors who journeyed to Osborne did not see the Queen. She sat in an adjoining room to them, with the door half open, and the meeting's business was transacted in addresses to the empty doorway, with the sovereign's responses relayed from the other room. Nevertheless, in an echo of her words on her accession in 1835, she had said even on the night of her husband's death that 'They [the politicians] need not be afraid. I will do my duty.' She could not give up her position: she and her role as monarch were a unity. No king or queen of England had ever abdicated voluntarily, and she had no intention of being the first. It is likely that the demands of her position in fact gave her something to cling to in a sea of desolation. Besides, her vacation of the throne would mean the accession of Bertie as King. That was unthinkable. Quite apart from his youth, inexperience, and untrustworthiness, it was her view, encouraged by Sir James Clark, who had referred to Albert's 'excessive mental excitement on one very recent occasion' as one of the causes of his death, that the Curragh episode had led directly to the Prince's death. Bertie was to blame. His mother made little secret of this belief, and 1862 was an extremely difficult year for the Prince of Wales. Though at the end of January 1862 she told Palmerston that Bertie was 'a good and dutiful son', there were sometimes moments when she seemed to regard him with little short of horror. He bore it all with exemplary loyalty and forbearance.

Thoughts of Albert, and plans for the appropriate commemoration of the Prince, were Victoria's main considerations as 1862 went on. She determined to build a mausoleum in Frogmore Gardens, close to her mother's last home in Windsor Great Park, where he could be interred and where her coffin would in due time join his. His letters and speeches would be published; a 'Life' would be written. A grand memorial would be built in London, in that 'Albertopolis' district of great museums in South Kensington which owed so much to his powers of planning and organisation: a monument and a vast circular hall. His rooms at Windsor, Osborne, and Balmoral were to be kept just as they were, as shrines and perhaps more, for she genuinely appears to have believed in his spiritual proximity and it was thus only appropriate to keep his apartments available. Fresh towels were put out twice daily; changes of clothes laid out; warm water run into the washbasins.

Victoria was also determined from the start of her new life that Albert should be perpetuated in another way, in that his views and rules would forever be hers. On Christmas Eve 1861, she confided this to Leopold:

'I am also anxious to repeat *one* thing, and *that one* is my *firm* resolve, my *irrevocable decision*, viz. that *his* wishes – *his* plans – about everything, his views about *every* thing are to be *my law!* And *no human power* will make me swerve from what *he* decided and wished – and I look to *you* to *support* and *help* me in this. I apply this particularly as regards our children – Bertie, etc., – for whose future he had traced everything so carefully. I am *also determined* that *no one* person, may he be ever so good, ever so devoted among my servants – is to lead or guide or dictate to *me*. I know how *he* would disapprove it.'

Old echoes ring in that last assertion, even of Leopold's own one-time attempt to use her influence, though it is very unlikely that he was being aimed at this time. He was the senior member of the Coburg family and she badly wanted his moral support. The Queen grasped the fact that she was vulnerable, both as a woman and a monarch. Her years of seclusion, usually put down only to exaggerated and self-indulgent mourning for Albert, also owe something to this intense resolve not to offer any opportunity to be dominated or directed. Sir John Conroy, who had died embittered in 1854, never having received the peerage he craved and which Melbourne had promised, was not forgotten by Victoria.

Gradually, what Lytton Strachey called 'the violence of her perturbations' subsided, but the Queen's cheerfulness seemed to be buried with her husband. Mourning persisted, and an atmosphere of sombre gloom pervaded the court and her homes. Just over a year after Albert's death, on 17 December 1862, the Bishop of Oxford consecrated the domed mausoleum to which Albert's coffin was taken from St George's Chapel in Windsor Castle. A recumbent statue of the Prince was made, and the same sculptor, Marochetti, made a companion one of the Queen for future use. The monuments appeared, rather more slowly. Between 1863 and 1876, Sir Gilbert Scott and a team of craftsmen worked on the Albert Memorial. The great Royal Albert Hall, designed by Francis Fowke, did not get under way until 1867 and was opened by the Queen in 1871. Her aim was that the people should understand what they owed to the Prince, but neither construction was completed by public subscription alone. Parliament voted £50,000 to the memorial;

the Hall had to become the commercial venture of a joint-stock company.

As 1862 merged into 1863, it became clear to her counsellors, ministers, and subjects that Queen Victoria had no intention of emerging from her mourning state. Respect for her loss and acceptance of the need for a period of mourning began to be replaced by a sense of impatience. The business of state had to be resumed. It was expected that Victoria would take up her public and ceremonial role, after a reasonable interval. Such assumptions were not shared by the Queen herself. To her, being Queen was not a matter of external show: it was a sacramental condition laid upon her, not through her own choice, not by popular election, but because of her birth, and that could only be ended at her death. It was a glory and a burden that Divine Providence had selected her for. That condition implied duties and responsibilities, but in the end, how she carried them out was up to her. That, at any rate, was how she saw it.

Her ministers viewed her functions as being more within the form of the British constitution than that of divine ordainment. The compact between monarchy and Parliamentary government, that had sustained the country since 1688, worked best when the king or queen was visible, public, and active. An unseen monarch, living in seclusion, hidden in palace or castle, was an un-British notion, giving rise to all kinds of undesirable ideas. At a time when the common people had more political power and involvement than ever before (and many were campaigning for more), it suggested a dislike or distrust of her subjects on the Queen's part. To some it suggested that she was plotting in secret to increase her own power, to create an authoritarian monarchy of the kind that was now emerging in Prussia. To others, remembering the Regency period, the issue seemed quite straightforward. Either the Queen was capable of doing her job, or she wasn't. If she wasn't, then it was the duty of her doctors and advisers to say so, and make other arrangements. After all, there was a Prince of Wales, young, hale, and by all accounts hearty, able to take a more prominent public role.

There were also many who defended the Queen, sometimes unexpectedly. One of her supporters was the Radical and reformist politician, John Bright, who spoke out in her defence in 1866:

> 'I think there has been, by many persons, a great injustice done to the Queen in reference to her desolate widowed position, and I venture to say this, that a woman, be she the Queen of a great realm, or be she the wife of one of your labouring men, who can keep active in her heart a great sorrow for the lost object of her life and affection, is not at all likely to be wanting in great and generous sympathy with you.'

Any hint here of male superiority to the emotional feebleness of womanhood was lost on the Queen, who felt that Bright was among the very few men of affairs who understood her situation.

To the Queen, her burden and responsibility fell into two separate areas. One was the ceremonial aspect of monarchy, the drawing-room and other receptions, the attendance at military parades and fleet reviews, audiences with foreign ambassadors, and so on, and of course the State Opening of Parliament, which she had dreaded even at the best of times. The other, and to her far more important aspect, was the executive role of the monarch in supervising, monitoring, and contributing to the work of government and affairs of state generally, but most especially in foreign affairs. This role was one she never shirked. She insisted that all policy documents, letters, and despatches be provided to her as before, and set herself to the now solitary task of dealing with them as Albert had taught her. They had to be read, considered, and annotated, approved, or referred back. Nothing could be signed before she had read it and considered its import. Since she often felt unable to have face-to-face meetings with ministers, much of the discussion was carried on by letter, both more laborious and time-consuming. She rarely came to London, and those ministers who were obliged to present themselves had to travel out to Windsor, and very often to Osborne or Balmoral.

In the summer of 1862, it became clear to politicians that Victoria's physical seclusion had by no means lessened her sense of involvement with political life – in fact it added a new dimension. Knowing that Palmerston's government was precarious, she wrote privately to the Tory leader, Lord Derby, to inform him that she was not in a fit state to contemplate a change of government, and that if Palmerston were forced out of government, it would endanger her very life. The aged Palmerston continued in office until his death in 1865, to be briefly succeeded by Lord Russell until Derby and the Tories won the general election in 1866.

Most of her subjects thought the Queen was doing nothing – this was the most damaging aspect of her desire for seclusion. The only public ceremonies that she performed were the unveilings of statues to the Prince Consort. These were also erected in many places where the Queen never went: a statue of 'Albert the Good' still stands in Sydney, Australia. But she was very busy. Quite apart from state papers, the appointments to bishoprics, regius professorships, and all the other official matters, there was the family. Two marriages were in the offing. Alice's to Prince Louis of Hesse-Darmstadt, and, more portentously, Bertie's to Princess Alexandra of Denmark. Albert's view had been that marriage would have a steadying influence on the Prince of Wales, but that clearly depended on whom he married. The next Queen must be as perfect a consort as her husband (his parents earnestly hoped and prayed) would be a perfect king. It took two years of scanning the ranks of suitably Protestant and Germanic princesses before Vicky and Victoria came up with the seventeen-year-old Alexandra. Her Danishness and her family connections with the raffish Hesse-Cassel princely family, were at first held against her, but when Victoria, in her first journey abroad since Albert's death, met her at Leopold's palace in Brussels, the Queen was won over. Bertie had been introduced to Alix, as she was called, in

The Making of a Widow

September 1861, and had expressed enthusiasm for the match. Now, in September 1862, he was summoned to Brussels and allowed to propose. The young couple appear to have been genuinely attracted to each other, but Victoria left no doubt that the important thing was that the bride-to-be suited her. Alix was invited to Osborne to stay with the Queen while her fiancé took a Mediterranean cruise with Vicky and her husband Fritz. Victoria continued to be delighted with the girl, and wrote to Vicky to thank her for discovering a 'jewel ... she is so dear, so gentle, good, simple, unspoilt – so thoroughly honest and straight forward – so affectionate.' Alix would remain a favourite and her arrival in the family helped to ease the relationship between Bertie and his mother. But she would not countenance any involvement by Bertie in sharing her burden, and he was completely excluded from state affairs.

Alice's wedding to Louis of Hesse-Darmstadt, solemnised on 1 July 1862 in the dining-room at Osborne, was the first festive event in the royal family since Albert's death, but it was a very subdued affair. Bertie's wedding, on 10 March 1863, had necessarily to be a grander affair, but the spirit of mourning still prevailed. For Albert's widow, the prime thing about it was that he was not there. It took place in St George's Chapel, Windsor, and the Queen sat secluded in Katherine of Aragon's closet, having expressed the hope that there would be no excessive 'noise and joyousness'. Immediately after the ceremony, she went to visit the Mausoleum. Nothing would be allowed to lighten the atmosphere of determined gloom that enshrouded her as completely as the inevitable black dress which clad her buxom figure.

Bertie and Alix had a London home in Marlborough House, and a country estate at Sandringham in Norfolk, but they were not free from Victoria's close and interfering interest. She was as domineering a mother-in-law as she was a mother. Though she could not prevent the Prince and Princess of Wales from adopting a position as leaders of 'Society' and participants in the London 'Season' in a way in which Albert and she had never sought or desired, she did her best to control their lives and their circle of friends and acquaintances. It was said that they could not dine out except at houses approved by the Queen, and had to submit their own guest lists for her approval. Alix proved her value in the dynastic sense by producing a son, Albert Victor, in January 1864, and another, George, in June 1865. Three daughters followed in the next three years. A loyal wife to an errant husband, she also provided the 'even keel' that Victoria and Albert had hoped for; and she became a favourite with the London crowd.

Among her homes, it was Balmoral where the Queen found most solace. She longed for the summer when she could remove to there, and hated the time of late autumn when she had to return to Windsor and the ceremonies of state. She retreated to it in May 1862, with Alice and Alfred, and at first was deeply stricken by a new onrush of grief, in the castle Albert had designed, and which seemed so full of his spirit and the memories of unrecoverable happy times. Not for the first time, a kind of self-regard is detectable in her wailing to Vicky, for all its undoubted sincerity.

> 'Oh! darling child, the agonising sobs as I crawled up with Alice and Affie! The stags' heads – the rooms – blessed, darling Papa's room – then his coats – his caps – kilts – all, all convulsed my poor shattered frame!'

But in the course of the summer, the effects of open air, the Highland scenery, the old affection for the Highland people, the sense of remoteness from the world of politics and diplomacy, all had a beneficial effect.

Was it only a profound but natural grief that afflicted Victoria through 1862 and indeed for a decade to come, or was it something more akin to what nowadays would be called a nervous breakdown? Even in an age when mourning was formal and serious, particularly for the wealthy who had both the time and the money to practise it, the Queen's reaction began to seem extravagant after six months or so. As usual, silence and invisibility prompted speculation and gossip, and it was frequently said that she had gone mad. Once again the example of George III was trotted out. Extreme grief can, of course, itself produce or prompt various side effects. Lack of sleep, loss of appetite, lack of exercise, all have their own impact on mental and physical well-being. The afflicted person can be locked into a downhill progress in which cause and effect form an ever-extending chain. In the early stages of her mourning, some of these aspects were shown by the Queen. Observers remarked that she looked thin and worn. She herself complained of headaches and a sense of lassitude such that she could hardly walk. In the summer of 1862, she herself seemed to feel that too much pressure might unhinge her brain; hence the plea to Lord Derby; and Lord Clarendon reported that she had told him she feared going mad on three occasions while at Balmoral. She thought of her own death as a welcome release, and more than a quarter of a century later, confessed to Vicky that she had even thought of suicide, 'but a Voice told me for His sake – no, "Still Endure".' And endure she did, protecting herself by establishing a set routine for the days, weeks, months – eventually years – that lay before her.

It might have been expected that the Queen would also seek solace in trying to establish spiritual contact with her dead husband. This was very common in the nineteenth century, and persons of greater intellectual stature than Victoria were prepared to give credence to mediums, spirit voices, automatic writing, and all the other manifestations of contact between this world and the great Beyond. There were rumours at the time that she did do so, often linked to John Brown, perhaps through hazy notions of the Second Sight as a special gift of Highlanders. One of her biographers, Lady Longford, explored these suggestions without finding any evidence for them. There is no doubt that the Queen continued to feel the presence of Albert close to her; but that was quite different from the table-tapping in darkened rooms which so many others believed in.

Her role as head of the Church may have helped the Queen to steer clear of the wilder shores of spiritualism, but she might also be given credit for a fundamental common sense in the matter.

While Victoria set up, and saw, her rigid routine as a protection against the outside world, it was also a protection against her deep inner self and the demons that lurked there. She rationalised it in a different way. To cope with every demand was impossible – therefore she would restrict herself to what she considered most vital, her non-public duties as Queen and the management of her own household. This was a very substantial workload in itself. Public appearances were not vital; they were fatiguing and emotionally draining. They could be dispensed with. There were two sides to a public appearance, however: the other being the public itself. Victoria's subjects did not like to be dispensed with. They neither knew nor cared that the Queen worked long hours at her desk. They suspected that the Queen could not be bothered to make even occasional public appearances. Some of those closer to her shared the same view. General Charles Grey, who had been Albert's Private Secretary after Anson's death and remained in the court circle, believed that she was a 'Royal Malingerer' who was simply exploiting the opportunity to do what she liked, and ignore what she didn't like. He felt she had yielded to her own whims, and ought to take a grip on herself. Even hinting at such a course to the Queen, however, brought her into a state of feverish indignation in which all the symptoms of nervous debility returned. She had headaches, nausea, insomnia, and fatigue; she even complained of feeling the cold – all of it compounded by the feeling that no one really understood what and how she suffered. In 1862, Sir William Jenner succeeded Clark as her Physician in Ordinary, but he did nothing to discourage her attitude. The Queen could always count on Jenner to confirm that what she most needed was rest, preferably in the bracing air of Deeside, and freedom from worry. He became a rather favoured courtier, with influence in the royal household beyond his strictly medical remit, and some of his colleagues felt that this affected his diagnoses. Another courtier, Colonel Phipps, wrote to Palmerston in 1863 to say:

> 'Her Majesty's Physicians are very decidedly of opinion that with a due regard to the preservation of Her Majesty's health ... it would be highly undesirable for her to appear in state on public occasions.'

A regular change of air was, however, considered beneficial to the Queen, and in late 1862 she travelled to Germany, to make a visit to Coburg, the first of three in the course of the next three years. She broke her journey to visit King Leopold, now seventy-two and becoming frail. She called on Baroness Lehzen, whom she had not seen since 1845, though they had written to each other. In 1863 on her second visit, she had a short meeting with the Austrian Emperor, Franz Josef, thirteen years her junior, and who almost uniquely among the crowned heads of Europe, would have a longer reign than her own. (He occupied the Habsburg throne from 1848 to 1916.) On her third visit, in 1865, she unveiled a statue of Albert in the marketplace of Coburg, the sole public duty she found congenial.

The strong-willed child had grown up into a woman whose word was law, and knew it, and had no hesitation in exploiting it. Within her family, the Prince Consort alone had been able to exercise some constraint on his wife. Her imperious nature did not relish opposition even from him. Conflict of wills prompted their rare disagreements. In 1893, she wrote to a granddaughter:

> 'So many girls think to marry is *merely* to be independent and amuse oneself – whereas it is the very *reverse* of independence – 2 wills have to be *made* to act together and it is *only* by *mutual* agreement and *mutual yielding* to one another that a happy marriage can be arrived at.'

She had written to Vicky about Albert in critical terms more than once in the year before his death. On one occasion he had compelled her to come to London when she had wanted to stay at Windsor because their son, Leopold, was ill. 'I am very much annoyed and distressed at being forced to leave him by the very person who ought to wish me to stay.' In September she wrote of Albert:

> 'He has his faults too. He is very often very trying – in his hastiness and over-love of business – and I think you would find it very trying if Fritz was as hasty and harsh (momentarily and unintentionally as it is) as he is!'

Such episodes were forgotten in the subsequent cult of Albert the Good, but, more importantly, there was now no constraint. With Albert, she could be Queen and woman. Now, with her femininity discounted (she never for a moment considered the possibility of remarriage), and no one to counter her whims or challenge her impulses, she became a monster. Possessiveness, self-pity, self-deception about her own condition, and a hysterical inability to bear criticism, were the hallmarks of her life at this time. Were it not for the fact that Charles Dickens had written David Copperfield in 1850, one might feel that he had his widowed sovereign in mind with the character of Mrs Gummidge: 'I am a lone, lorn creetur ... and everythink goes contrairy with me.' The Queen's own words were: 'I am on a dreary sad pinnacle of solitary grandeur.'

How seriously she continued to view her duty was evident in the European crisis which blew up at the end of 1863 – the 'Schleswig-Holstein Question'. These two duchies, in the neck of the Jutland peninsula between Denmark and Germany, had been administered by Denmark. On the death of King Frederick of Denmark, and the accession of Christian IX (Princess Alexandra's father) in November, they had been occupied by Prussia (whose king, William, was Vicky's father-in-law). War broke out between Denmark and Prussia, the latter also supported by Austria. British public sympathy was with Denmark, as was that of Palmerston's government, but there was no general urge for war. Prussia was a former ally, and there had been no long build-up of rivalry and hostility, as there was to be in the years prior to 1914. Remembering Albert's vision of Prussia as the leader of a liberal and enlightened German union, the Queen was wholly in favour of Prussia, and was greatly upset by the pro-Danish views of her Prime Minister and Foreign Secretary. Missives were sped to and from the various royal residences, Downing Street, and the Foreign Office. They contained the Queen's comments, demands for information, complaints, and appeals on the one side, and the official replies expressing the opposite point of view on the other. All of which filled her with frustration and anger. She did not spare herself, and took pains to let them know that she was not sparing herself:

> 'The Queen suffers much, and her nerves are more and more totally shattered .... The Queen is completely exhausted by the anxiety and suspense, and misses her beloved husband's help, advice, support and love in an overwhelming manner.'

But the flow of messages never stopped. She was also writing to her relatives in Germany, but despite her ardour in support of Prussia, she strove to be noncommittal to them, knowing that, in the end, if her government decided to assist Denmark, there was nothing she could do to stop it. But the British government remained neutral.

Her own family was divided. Bertie took the part of Denmark, as did Alix. Vicky's husband was with the Prussian army. The Prince of Wales made his support for Denmark so obvious that the Prussian ambassador made an official protest. A new rift opened between the Queen and her heir, not merely because of this difference of opinion but because of the Prince's indiscretion in blurting out his views. To Victoria this confirmed his immaturity and unfitness to be involved with matters of state. For a time, too, 'darling Alix' became identified as an enemy within the walls. There were numerous claimants to rule Schleswig, Holstein, or both, including Prince Frederick of Augustenburg, who was married to Feodora's daughter, Adelaide. Feodora, Victoria's half-sister, was a guest at Windsor when the crisis blew up. As a supporter of her son-in-law's claim, she and the Princess of Wales were in fierce disagreement. The distracted Victoria forbade any mention of the issue.

The Prussian-Austrian victory and annexation of the duchies put an end to the Augustenburgs' and others' dreams. It also began to change Queen Victoria's views. With Otto von Bismarck as Prime Minister, it was plain that, although Prussia was indeed now intent on unifying Germany under its leadership, it was not brandishing a liberal beacon but an authoritarian sword. Though Vicky and Fritz had loyally supported the Danish war, their Albertian liberalism was completely marginalised and Vicky herself was deeply unpopular, both for her own opinions and because of Britain's neutrality and her brother's partisanship for Denmark. The Queen had been wrong to trust Prussia and had supported it for the wrong reasons. Albert might have been flexibly minded enough to see the true facts. For Victoria, it was enough that Albert in previous years had been pro-Prussian. She did not realise that her effort to emulate Albert's example was impossible. However diligently she laboured at her papers, she was living in the past and could neither see nor understand the way in which Europe was changing.

As work began, and very slowly continued, on Albert's monument in South Kensington, Victoria was considering other ways in which his memory could be preserved. Overwhelmed by her own sense of loss, she wanted the British people to understand what an incomparable figure they, too, had lost. Perhaps she also wanted them to feel regret that during his lifetime they had not been more appreciative of his qualities. In 1862, a substantial collection of the Prince's speeches was published, so that his words would be permanently available. General Grey was commissioned to write an account of Albert's early years, up to the time of his marriage. The Queen, of course, took a great interest in the preparation of *The Early Years of the Prince Consort*, supplying the General with a great deal of material, but also keeping a close eye on what he wrote. This was completed in 1866 and published in 1867. Grey was unable to write the intended second volume, and this task was entrusted to Theodore Martin, a genial Scottish lawyer and amateur man of letters, who had a lucrative practice as Parliamentary agent for a number of railway companies. The practice was increasingly neglected as the scale of his task became clear. *The Life of HRH The Prince Consort* was eventually published in five volumes between 1875 and 1880. Martin, too, received what Lytton Strachey ironically referred to as 'the gracious assistance of Her Majesty'. She was an avid editor, striking out what she regarded as unnecessarily critical; or adding little notes of justification. If the author should write that Albert found palace balls and dances tedious affairs, the royal annotator would insert a note that, nevertheless, he would have a kind word for everyone there, and sometimes remain on his feet all evening in his dedication to duty. Supervision of these literary projects was for her a labour of love. Unfortunately, the books found little success with the public, and she was surprised and hurt by the reaction. Her monomania was not shared by her subjects. Lytton Strachey summed matters up:

> 'Victoria's emotional nature, far more remarkable
> for vigour than for subtlety, rejecting utterly the
> qualifications which perspicacity, or humour, might
> suggest, could be satisfied with nothing but the absolute
> and the categorical. When she disliked she did so with
> an unequivocal emphasis which swept the object of
> her repugnance at once and finally outside the pale
> of her recognition; and her feelings of affection were
> equally unmitigated. In the case of Albert her passion

for superlatives reached its height. To have conceived of him as anything short of perfect – perfect in virtue, in wisdom, in beauty, in all the glories and graces of man – would have been an unthinkable blasphemy; perfect he was, and perfect he must be shown to have been. And so Sir Arthur [Arthur Helps, editor of the speeches], Sir Theodore and the General painted him.'

The books were long, worthy, boring, and generally dismissed as one-sided and excessively flattering to their subject. Though Martin was rewarded with a knighthood, a 'warts-and-all' portrait of the Prince would have done far more to engrave and endear his memory among the public. His widow, however, was totally incapable of seeing this. Curiously, she achieved much greater success with a book she wrote on her own. Delving back into her journals – still regularly kept – she compiled *Leaves from the Journal of Our Life in the Highlands*. She had even compelled herself to return to the day of Albert's death in order to keep the record complete. Published in 1868 and dedicated to Albert's memory, its portrait of him was no less sugary and unreal than that in the biographies, but its revelations of the royal family's simple pleasures at Balmoral, and the inevitable and often unintended glimpses of Victoria's own artless and straightforward nature, were eagerly consumed by the public. No English monarch had ever published an autobiographical book before, and thousands of readers were keen to vicariously share the daily lives of the royal family. Even among the staunchly republican citizens of the USA, it became a bestseller. Delighted by the reception, Victoria wrote in her diary that 'I am known and understood.' She felt it made a bond between her and her people.

Leaves was a double pleasure for the Queen to write, as it combined her two loves, the dead Albert and the still-inspiring Highlands. It was noted that the atmosphere of gloom, which attended all her appearances and functions, was noticeably lightened at her Scottish home. Balmoral was to her a safe and protective environment in which her almost phobic aversion to being a public spectacle could be forgotten. She could 'drop in' on cottagers who lived on the royal estate, who would welcome her as they might the laird's wife, with respect and interest, but without obsequiousness or social embarrassment. In such company, she could forget her 'pinnacle of solitary grandeur'. At the annual Ghillies Ball, she would sit up late to watch the tartans whirl in the reels, and listen to the bagpipes, apparently oblivious to the fact that around her whisky was being consumed in spectacular quantities. But then she never was a supporter of the movement for total abstinence from alcohol, any more than she was a Sabbatarian. These two typically 'Victorian' causes got no encouragement from the Queen, who thought they went too far.

The Balmoral outdoor servants remained at Balmoral and only the Queen's personal maid, Annie Macdonald, accompanied her everywhere. But in October 1864, Dr Jenner and Colonel Phipps arranged to bring down to Osborne her 'faithful Highland servant' who so reliably looked after her on outings into the mountains. They wanted to encourage her to resume riding, which she had refused to do since Albert's death. The experiment was a success. John Brown soon had the Queen riding again, while his strong hand held the leading rein. Then aged thirty-eight, he quickly became a vital and indispensable member of the royal household. He was designated as 'The Queen's Highland Servant', and she required his attendance ...

> '... ALWAYS and everywhere out of doors, whether riding or driving or on foot; and it is a *real* comfort, for he is *so* devoted to me – so simple, so intelligent, so unlike an *ordinary* servant, and so cheerful and attentive.'

Brown was a strong and sturdy figure, whose strength, quickness of action and protective instinct would serve the Queen well more than once. But his society for her was a constant tonic, as he, invariably kilted, and with a rich Grampian burr in his voice, seemed to bring the heathery hills and fresh breezes of her favourite place with him. He served her without a break until his death in 1883.

Two deaths in 1865 enhanced Victoria's sense of her increasing age and solitude. One was that of Palmerston, who died at eighty-one while still Prime Minister and shortly after winning an election. His government, since 1859, with William Ewart Gladstone as Chancellor of the Exchequer, had maintained the tradition of Peel in a range of reforms to the British financial system and in extending the principle of Free Trade. Now, though Lord Russell succeeded him as Premier, the key figure in the Liberal Party was Gladstone. On the Conservative side, though Derby was still leader, the coming man was Disraeli. Both of these eminent future prime ministers were older than the Queen: in 1865, Disraeli was sixty-one and Gladstone was fifty-seven. Despite their differences, most recently over the Schleswig-Holstein crisis, Victoria had felt comfortable with Palmerston, whom she had known for so long.

The other death had struck her more closely; her Uncle Leopold, for so many years a father-substitute and confidant, died at the age of seventy-five. In grief or in glory, he had been the first person, Albert apart, that she turned to; now she herself was the central figure in the network of Coburg family relationships. The network was still extending, as further weddings took place. In July 1866, Princess Helena (Lenchen) married a German prince whose title was as long as his purse was short, Christian of Schleswig-Holstein-Sonderburg-Augustenburg. Again the Danish-German duchies would cause a rift in the British royal family. Though Christian, as a younger son, had no claim on Schleswig-Holstein or anywhere else, Bertie's Danish sympathies were aroused again. He and Alice opposed the marriage, much to their mother's fury. In some of her last letters to Uncle Leopold, Victoria deplored Alice's behaviour:

> 'Alice (to my great sorrow for she used to be such a comfort to me) is very unamiable and altogether not changed to her advantage. But the contrary in many ways – sharp and grand and wanting to have everything her own way.'

In the Queen's view, there was only one person who ought to have everything her own way, and that was certainly not Alice. Once she had established that Christian was agreeable to living in England, her enthusiasm for Lenchen's marriage was greatly increased. If Vicky was perforce in Prussia, and Alice partly escaped to Hesse (from where she was frequently summoned back to Britain), Lenchen would still be close by to provide the company and consolation of a loyal daughter to a bereaved, grieving, and determinedly possessive mother. To ensure that proximity, Christian was appointed to the governorship of Windsor Castle.

In July 1866, the royal families of Europe were distressed and confused by the short, sharp war mounted by Prussia against Imperial Austria. This was the culminating stroke of Bismarck's policy to establish the supremacy of Prussia within Germany, and to marginalise Austria. Once again Vicky's husband was in command of a Prussian army corps in action. Alice's husband, Louis, had mobilised the slender forces of Hesse-Darmstadt in alliance with Austria, and shared in the Empire's humiliating defeat. Within seven weeks, all was over, and Prussia was triumphant. Alice had the discomfiture of seeing Vicky's country seizing part of her own as part of the peace settlement.

Britain again remained neutral during this conflict, although the Queen pressed Russell to intervene against Prussia. The change in the power structure within Europe was baffling to British politicians of both parties, with the rise of a dynamic and powerful Germany upsetting all previous notions of the 'balance of power'. In 1866, Russell dissolved Parliament and called a general election, which was won by the Conservatives.

Derby became Prime Minister and Disraeli, Chancellor of the Exchequer. Once again his was the hand that wrote the daily account of Parliamentary proceedings. In former times, Victoria had no liking for Disraeli. She had detested his hounding of Peel and his opposition to Free Trade. She knew that Albert had considered him a shallow and opportunistic politician, 'with not one single element of the gentleman in his composition'. But, in his first stint as Leader of the Commons, she had been impressed and intrigued, against her will, by the style of his reports, which had a personal, unofficial flavour which made them much more pleasantly readable than most of the government papers she saw. What won her over completely was Disraeli's appreciation of Albert's character and his empathy for her sense of loss. Alone among her statesmen, she felt he truly understood and mourned the greatness of Albert. From the terrible days of December 1861, he had seized on this theme and never ceased to play it to the Queen. From the Opposition benches, he had spoken eloquently in favour of a Parliamentary grant towards a national memorial to the Prince, and had afterwards received a specially bound copy of Albert's speeches, inscribed by the Queen and accompanied by a letter which praised his tribute 'to her adored, beloved and great husband. The perusal of it made her shed many tears, but it was very soothing to her broken heart.' Disraeli's reply was fulsome, writing in the same stately third-person mode that was deemed appropriate for royal correspondence:

> 'The Prince is the only person whom Mr Disraeli has
> ever known who realised the Ideal. None with whom
> he is acquainted have ever approached it. There was in
> him a union of the manly grace and sublime simplicity,
> of chivalry with the intellectual splendour of the Attic
> Academe. The only character in English history that
> would, in some respects, draw near to him is Sir
> Philip Sidney; the same high tone, the same universal
> accomplishment, the same blended tenderness and

vigour, the same rare combination of romantic energy and classic repose.'

Acquaintance with the Prince had been 'one of the most satisfactory incidents of his life; full of refined and beautiful memories, and exercising, as he hopes, over his remaining existence, a soothing and exalting influence.' This was such stuff as Victoria could have read all day and still have hungered for more. Like herself, Disraeli did not do things by halves. He had had a genuine regard and respect for the Prince Consort's achievement, and all his very considerable psychological insight and mental dexterity were summoned to make the highest degree of appeal to the Queen. His tributes succeeded because they were not mere vapid gush, but picked out and delineated aspects of her husband's character that she herself could not have articulated so well. Through the prism held up by Disraeli, she could see Albert's virtues in new and pleasing ways.

One might ask why he bothered. Queen Victoria's opinion of him would hardly matter if he, as leader of the Conservative Party – which he fully intended to become – should win a general election. She would have to ask him to form her government. There were, however, political considerations: the result of an election might not be clear cut, the Queen, with her advisors, might have to choose. Minority governments were frequent. To enjoy the Queen's favour would do no harm and perhaps some good. But these were secondary considerations: Disraeli's romantic nature genuinely did empathise with the widowed Victoria. In a curious way, they were both 'outsiders': she on her lonely pinnacle, and he, Jewish-born, baptised at twelve, aspiring to, and finally reaching, the top of what he famously described as 'the greasy pole' of British political life, without ever feeling himself to be part of the country's 'Establishment'.

To Disraeli, the Queen was first and foremost a person, a character to be appreciated, adored, and flattered, a woman who was monarch of a great nation, a regal person who yet was vulnerable and bore a crippling loss. To his intimates, he referred to her as 'the Faery', as if she were some kind of half-supernatural sprite. To his great contemporary and political rival, William Ewart Gladstone, Victoria was above all the embodiment of a great, enduring, and sacred national institution, the monarchy. In the presence of his sovereign, or in communicating with her, he felt her womanhood, if he considered it at all, as a distinctly minor consideration. He had been Albert's friend and the Prince had admired him, but Gladstone's condolences were formal and impersonal compared to Disraeli's. Gladstone shared Palmerston's view that the Queen ought to pull herself together and resume her life; and Victoria knew it. She also suspected that Gladstone did not consider her indispensable. He certainly tolerated the presence of out-and-out republicans in his own party, men like Sir Charles Dilke and Joseph Chamberlain, who would send the House of Saxe-Coburg-Gotha back to Germany and install some frock-coated politician in Buckingham Palace as head of state. Gladstone was not remotely republican in his own sympathies, but there was never any human warmth in his relations with the Queen.

Early in 1868, Lord Derby resigned as Prime Minister and Victoria had the pleasure of inviting Mr Disraeli to form her government. It was a minority administration, under constant threat of toppling, and defeat on 1 May on the Irish Church question forced him to offer his resignation. In the end, as new electoral registers were in preparation, he maintained his minority government until December, when he was decisively ousted in a general election. The nine months of Disraeli's first government were greatly enjoyed by the Queen. Not since Lord Melbourne's day had audiences with her Prime Minister been such an agreeable experience, and this time the relationship was not that of worldly-wise teacher and novice pupil, but that of a mature and knowledgeable Queen and her deferential but understanding, sympathetic, and perceptive first minister. His letters, too, were a source of pleasure, combining information, background details, and helpful clarifications with a spice of news and gossip. The delighted Queen, for the first time since Albert's death, felt that she was being told everything. The ties of personal friendship soon underlay the warm official relationship. That spring, bunches of primroses, picked by her in Windsor Park, were sent to 10 Downing Street, and thanks were returned in the Prime Minister's inimitable fashion, telling her that 'their lustre was enhanced by the condescending hand which had showered upon him all the treasures of Spring.'

But in December, defeat in Parliament forced Disraeli to call a general election, which the Liberals won, and Gladstone became Prime Minister for the first time. The full term of a Parliament was then seven years, and it seemed likely that she would have to do without Disraeli for that time. It soon became clear that in various ways the new Premier's approach to policy and to high appointments was at variance with the Queen's ideas. He had none of his rival's lightness of touch in introducing difficult or controversial topics, and was far more stubborn by nature – in this respect he matched Victoria herself. Both believed that God had put them in their respective positions for His own purposes and they should not let Him down.

Gladstone had come to power with a substantial reform programme, aspects of which caused great anxiety in the Queen's mind. The government wanted to disestablish the Church of Ireland, which was in effect a branch of the Church of England with a similar range of state privileges and functions, including entitlement to tithes from the whole population. The Church of Ireland was a minority church in a country overwhelmingly Roman Catholic but with a substantial Presbyterian population. As Head of the Church of Ireland, the Queen was gravely concerned; she wondered if her coronation oath, to uphold the Protestant religion, would allow her to sign such an Act. Changes to the administration of the Army were also being proposed. Up to this time, its command structure had been subordinate to a Commander-in-Chief, currently the Duke of Cambridge, who was appointed by, and responsible to, the sovereign. Gladstone's Liberal government now proposed to make the army's professional head subservient to Parliament, in the form of a Secretary for War. Even if the monarch's position as 'owner' of the Army had become a theoretical one, the Queen saw the change as an attack on her constitutional position and did her best to resist it until the Act of Parliament enabling it was passed. Conscious of the changes taking place in Europe, and of the devastating efficiency of the Prussian army, her government was taking belated steps towards reforming the antiquated structure of the British Army, but Victoria's vision was firmly set on the past. Albert and the Duke of Wellington (who had once suggested Albert as his successor in the post of Commander-in-Chief), she felt, would not have approved. Her cousin George, Duke of Cambridge, did not approve, and she was not going to approve either. But again she had to sign the Act. In another blow to tradition, the purchase of military commissions was abolished. Promotion of officers was now to be by merit. From many quarters a howl of protest went up about this importing of a 'professional' quality to the Army, not least from those who had paid for their commissions. The Queen was wholly on their side. She expected the House of Lords to throw out the measure, but the government, finding that the old system had been amended in 1809 by Royal Warrant, by-passed Parliament altogether and presented her with a Royal Warrant for its abolition. Reluctantly, she signed it, aware that in truth she was acknowledging the unchallengeable power of the government rather than asserting the power of the Crown. In response to her many expostulations, complaints, and queries, Gladstone dutifully and respectfully wrote back to her, but unlike Disraeli's letters, his were long, detailed, closely reasoned, and completely devoid of humour, by-the-way news items, and personal gossip. They frequently left her feeling bewildered and at a loss.

As shocks from outside continued, the regularity, ritual, and unchangeability of the Queen's routines became ever more important to her. For someone who was hostile to change, too many things were changing around her. She felt that the government was too extreme and hasty in its reformism. The news from Europe was rarely good, whether personal or political. Vicky's fourth child, Sigismund, died of meningitis in the summer of 1866 aged twenty-one months, causing her intense distress. But even within Victoria's own family at home, change and innovation could not be kept wholly at bay. Louise, twenty in 1868, and conscious of possessing both artistic talent and ambition, wanted to attend classes at the National Art Training School. Her mother grudgingly agreed to this, the first form of public education ever experienced by an English princess, though Louise's attendances were circumscribed by Victoria's frequent demands to have her at court or at home. By the time Louise was twenty-one, it also seemed high time that she was married. As with Lenchen, Victoria was determined that this daughter should continue to reside in Great Britain, in order to be near her, and when this prerequisite shortened the list of suitable continental princes to zero, the Queen herself initiated a novelty, by deciding that Louise could marry a British nobleman. No child of the monarch had married a subject since 1515, when Henry VII's daughter Elizabeth was married to the Duke of Suffolk, but Victoria's possessiveness and egotism, when fully aroused, could bulldoze through custom and tradition in a way that she would never have countenanced from anyone else. Several possible candidates were identified, but, given the Queen's appreciation of everything Highland, it was perhaps inevitable that her eye should fall on the handsome twenty-five year-old Marquess of Lorne, heir to the Duke of Argyll.

Continuance of a forceful role in government and family did not make Victoria any more visible to the general public, who continued to equate invisibility with inactivity. Taking tea with old ladies on the Balmoral estate was not enough. In 1864, she had taken the most unusual step of replying to criticism in The Times by writing, though not signing, a document which appeared in that newspaper and which blankly contradicted any suggestion that she might reappear in public:

> 'The Queen heartily appreciates the desire of her
> subjects to see her, and whatever she *can* do to gratify
> them in this loyal and affectionate wish, she *will* do ...
> but there are other and higher duties ... .'

This cut little ice even in 1864 and by the end of the decade the Queen's reclusiveness had become something in between a joke, a scandal, and an embarrassment for the nation. The success of *Leaves* did not establish the kind of rapport she had hoped for: only the middle class read it, and even they did not make the association she had hoped for, of understanding from descriptions of his life, what the death of her husband had done to her. 'What is she doing for her money?' was a favourite topic, along with 'If she can't do it, why doesn't she abdicate?'

'What Does She Do With It?' was the title of a widely circulated pamphlet, written anonymously by a clever young Radical, George Trevelyan, which examined the royal finances and revealed the fact that the Queen was not spending anything like the full Civil List annual payment of £328,000, and was actually saving and banking very large sums. This was not seen as respectable frugality but as a misuse of the taxpayers' money: in a sense the royal household, with its many ramifications and its high running costs, was an economic engine which helped to drive certain aspects of the economy, most of them in the luxury sector but involving a high standard of arts and crafts. To the Radicals, and to many who were not of strong radical views, the Queen was short-changing her people in a variety of ways.

If the Queen was invisible, however, in 1870, her eldest son became all too prominent. Bertie was far from being the model husband his father had been, and his affairs were well known in society circles. Although some of his biographers note that his respect for his mother seemed to extend into fear, there is little sign that her disapproval had any effect on his style of living. More than any of her other children, he had slipped the leash. In many ways, the horseplay and naughty behaviour of Marlborough House and Sandringham seem like the breaking-out of a repressed and over-disciplined child at last able to have his own way. Bertie's indulgences – horse racing, gambling, and adultery – were everything Albert had most deplored. But the convivial high spirits, the dancing, and the late nights of the Prince of Wales's set might have awakened at least an echo in the middle-aged Victoria of the pastimes of her early days as Queen. And he was quite prepared to stand up to her, at least by letter.

> 'I am always most anxious to meet your wishes in every respect, and always regret if we are not quite *d'accord*, but as I am past twenty-eight, and have some considerable knowledge of the world and society, you will I am sure, at least I trust, allow me to use my own discretion in matters of this kind.'

In the year he wrote this letter, however, Bertie's discretion slipped somewhat. He was called as a witness in a scandalous divorce case. Sir Charles Mordaunt's wife, Harriet, had confessed to him that she had had a number of prominent men as lovers, including the Prince of Wales. Letters from him were found in her desk, though they contained nothing to prove that she had been his mistress. Bertie was not incriminated though the Queen had no doubt that he was 'not innocent'. Caught between her family loyalty and her sense of reprobation, Victoria opted for the first and sent him a private message of support. The rise of republicanism and anti-monarchic feeling worried Gladstone. 'I cannot help continually revolving the question of the Queen's invisibility,' he told Lord Granville, ' ... in rude and general terms, the Queen is invisible and the Prince of Wales is not respected.'

Royalty and imperial pretension took a tumble in France in the autumn of 1870 when Bismarck's final moves towards Prussian supremacy were unveiled. The over-confident Emperor Napoleon III was provoked into declaring war on Prussia. Once again the British government preserved neutrality, but the Queen felt strongly engaged. Despite a personal admiration for Napoleon, she regarded his government as one of 'despotism, corruption, immorality, and aggression' and felt that his rapid and humiliating defeat and capture was an act of divine justice. Napoleon's Empress Eugénie fled to England, where Bertie (with chivalry, but also an impetuousness which his mother and the Foreign Secretary deplored) offered her the use of Chiswick House. In the midst of these tumultuous events, Victoria received news that Baroness Lehzen had died. 'My poor dear old Lehzen is gone to her rest, within less than a month of her eighty-sixth birthday! I owed her much and she adored me!' In March 1871, Napoleon III, released by the victorious Prussians, joined Eugénie as a refugee at Camden Place, Chislehurst. France was again a republic. But in January 1871, in the Hall of Mirrors at Versailles, King William of Prussia had been proclaimed as German Emperor. Vicky, as wife of the Crown Prince, could now aspire to a greater status than her mother.

For the first time since her husband's death, the Queen made an appearance at the State Opening of Parliament in 1871. It was a low-key occasion; clad as ever in black, she sat with an empty throne beside her, and the Speech from the Throne was read on her behalf by the Lord Chancellor. This half-hearted performance of a supposed annual duty did not win much praise. Public interest focused cynically on the fact that Parliament was being asked, by the Queen, to vote a dowry of £30,000, plus an annuity of £6000, from public funds to Princess Louise, whose engagement to the Marquess of Lorne had now been publicly announced. Later in the year, when Prince Arthur became of age, Parliament was asked to grant him an annuity of £15,000. The payments were granted but there was widespread indignation about 'princely paupers'. The estrangement between Crown and people was greater than at any point in Victoria's reign. In the Queen's view, it was everyone else's fault. To Theodore Martin, labouring patiently on his massive biography of the Prince Consort, she confided that she was 'a cruelly misunderstood woman' who felt almost driven to despair by 'the great worry and anxiety and hard work for ten years, alone, unaided, with increasing age and never very strong health.' As was once said of the Bourbons, Victoria, during that long and for her miserable decade, seemed to have learned nothing and forgotten nothing. Her failure to understand herself was as complete as her failure to understand others. Lytton Strachey remarked, 'If Victoria had died in the early seventies, there can be little doubt that the voice of the world would have pronounced her a failure.'

Louise's marriage was a further occasion for dispute between the Queen and the Prince of Wales. Bertie was not only opposed to it on grounds of custom and tradition; he also scored a shrewd hit by pointing out that since Lorne sat in the House of Commons as a Liberal MP, the wedding would drag the Crown into seeming to be politically partial – one of the things Albert had always been at pains to avoid. In court circles, where protocol and precedence were fussed over endlessly, a wife of greater rank than her husband was difficult to place. Bertie made much of this, perhaps forgetting that his mother had found herself in an exactly similar situation, and made it work successfully. The wedding took place in St George's Chapel, Windsor on 21 March 1871, with more pomp and circumstance than Lenchen's or Alice's wedding. Bertie stood beside his sister on the day, but she was given away by the Queen.

'Never very strong health' was a self-pitying delusion. The Queen was physically a healthy woman, a hearty eater with a sound digestion. Large meals and lack of exercise had made her overweight, increasing her portly girth. During her stay at Balmoral in 1871, however, she did become ill, and was diagnosed as having rheumatic gout and an axillary abscess. The abscess was removed by surgery, with the Queen again taking chloroform. Joseph Lister, then Regius Professor of Surgery at Glasgow, attended her, and used the carbolic anti-infection treatment that was to make him world-famous. Alice, on a visit from Germany, and currently restored to maternal favour, found herself in action as nurse, aided by Beatrice, now fourteen.

In December, ten years on from Albert's death, Bertie became gravely ill, with enteric fever. There was widespread concern and sympathy, accentuated in some circles by awareness that Bertie's son, Albert Victor, the next in line to Bertie as heir to the throne was only seven; and that the senior royal male would be Alfred ('Affie'), Duke of Edinburgh – a sailor prince of low morals with all the impatience, arrogance, and irascibility of his Hanoverian and Coburg ancestors. Bertie at least was affable and good-natured, though a stickler for punctuality in others. On his recovery, a service of thanksgiving was held in St Paul's Cathedral, attended by the Queen amidst a storm of public enthusiasm. She, too, had made a good recovery and resumed her by now time-honoured routines. That evening she appeared several times on the balcony to wave to the crowd gathered in front of the Palace. The effect of these two royal illnesses was to show how superficial the calls for a British republic were; and that even the more deep-seated grumbling about the Queen's behaviour was not remotely likely to bring the tumbrils to Buckingham Palace. Great Britain remained solidly monarchist. It was by an ironic twist of fate that a sixth apparent assassination attempt should be made now, just as she was beginning to re-emerge into public view. Two days after the service, as she drove in Hyde Park, a seventeen-year-old youth, Arthur O'Connor, slipped into the grounds of Buckingham Palace and menaced her, as she returned, with a pistol at close quarters. John Brown leapt from the carriage and collared him. It transpired that his pistol was unloaded, and he was trying to publicise the plight of Irish Fenian prisoners, but the Queen considered his twelve-month jail sentence far too light. To her doughty Highland Servant, however, her gratitude was immense.

Marriage-making was still important: Alfred and Arthur had yet to find brides; as for Beatrice, still so young – Victoria felt that it might be best for her not to marry at all. The other daughters, even Lenchen, whose home was at Windsor, had a tiresome habit of putting their husbands and families before their duty to their mother, and finding excuses for not attending on her. But Alfred arranged his own marriage, becoming engaged to the Grand Duchess Marie, daughter of the Russian Tsar, Alexander II. Neither Victoria nor the Tsar was greatly pleased. Affie had no great expectations (though in 1893 he became Duke of Saxe-Coburg-Gotha), and the Queen was distrustful of the Romanovs, partly because of Alexander's German alliance, and partly because of their Greek-Orthodox religion, which stirred her Protestant conscience as 'Defender of the Faith'. She wished to inspect the prospective daughter-in-law and bridled when the Tsar suggested, via Alice, she should come to Europe to do so. Alice received a stern rebuke:

> 'I do *not* think, dear Child, that you should tell me who have been nearly 20 *years longer* on the throne than the Emperor of Russia & am the Doyenne of Sovereigns … *what I ought to do.* I think I know *that.* The proposal received … was one of the *coolest* things I ever heard … .'

In the end there was no inspection. At Affie's wedding, in St Petersburg on 23 January 1874, Bertie represented the Queen. When Victoria finally met her new daughter-in-law, her reservations were forgotten, and Marie, like Alix, became a 'treasure'.

In 1874, Gladstone's long tenure of the premiership was decisively ended by a general election that returned the Tories with a large majority: their first majority government since 1841. Disraeli, now sixty-nine, kissed her hand as Prime Minister, much to her delight. Quite apart from her personal antipathy to Gladstone (despite his eloquent defence of the royal annuities), she had writhed under the Church of Ireland and Army reforms and felt generally that the Liberals were doing far too much. She resented Gladstone's reminders of duty. At the end of 1869, he was pressing his recalcitrant sovereign to open the new Blackfriars Bridge over the Thames in London, informing her that it was 'not given to any to occupy the Throne of the British Empire without special and heavy sacrifices.' She felt she already knew all about that. On that occasion, Gladstone won. In the summer of 1871, just before her serious illness, she had resisted fiercely when he had attempted to make her delay her departure for Balmoral until the Parliamentary session had come to an end. She had gone as planned. She had had enough of Gladstone, and it was a pleasure to find that the country now agreed with her. Gladstone resigned as leader of the Liberals and Lord Hartington assumed the role. When Disraeli had ceased to be Prime Minister in 1869, the Queen had shown her favour by making his wife a viscountess. Lady Beaconsfield died in 1873, and the Queen, from her own depths of experience, had condoled with the bereaved Disraeli. Now, despite the aristocratic confidantes so necessary for his self-esteem, there was only one woman in his life, his 'Faery'.

Once again the Queen felt she was being told everything, that she was at the centre of affairs, that things were done, not merely in her name, but with her active participation. 'Whatever your Majesty wishes shall be done,' Disraeli said in his first audience. If Victoria had taken him at his word, the results might have been interesting, but she was content for him to present plans and policies to her, for her consideration. Without preaching, or harangues, or appeal to her sense of duty, he got his way. From being treated simply as part of the apparatus of state, albeit the most august part, she was treated as if she were a monarch of endless powers – powers so great, so all-embracing, that there was really no need to dwell on them or go into their scope – and he, her Grand Vizier, intent only on executing her will. Dizzy (she referred to him by that name, as did everyone else) almost immediately resumed the close, cordial, and almost always harmonious relationship with Victoria that marked his first period in office, and kept it going until his defeat in the general election of 1880. It was a complex relationship, as fascinating to its two protagonists as it has been to later eavesdroppers. Deception, self-deception, trust, sincerity, even a kind of love all played a part in it, as well as a hard practicality. Deception, because Disraeli knew full well that power ultimately was with Parliament and whatever Her Majesty wished would not necessarily be done. Self-deception, because Victoria also knew that Parliament was supreme, but loved to feel that it was not, and Disraeli had a way of making it seem that Parliament was subservient to her will. Trust, because both were playing a game, in which he must trust her not to make impossible demands, and she must trust him not to place intolerable demands on her. Sincerity, because their feelings towards each other were genuine: she liked him, he admired, respected, and understood her: without that, his flatteries would have been transparent and useless. Disraeli was a far more artful, intelligent, and subtle-minded person than the Queen, but he never took her for granted and knew well that she could be formidable when roused. His great task was to keep her contented and tranquil, and in this, his chief weapon, as he admitted, was flattery. In a famous remark to Matthew Arnold, he said, 'You have heard me called a flatterer, and it is true. Everyone likes flattery; and when you come to royalty you should lay it on with a trowel.'

In as far as it was a game, both found it a delicious one and far more enjoyable than the conventional official relationship between Sovereign and Prime Minister. Yet at bottom, both saw things in practical terms. This was not a fantasy relationship: they were supervising the affairs of a large country, still facing huge social problems and opportunities undreamed of before; and beyond it a world of shifting powers, alliances, old enmities, and new partnerships. There was work to be done, and Disraeli's genius made the work a pleasure for both of them. Seven more years of Mr Gladstone, whatever it might have done for the country, would certainly have left Victoria a cantankerous and troublesome woman. (But she and Gladstone were far from done with each other yet, though both believed in 1874 that he had retired from the political fray.) Victoria was very much concerned to retain the powers of the Sovereign, even to reclaim some that had been lost. Disraeli was adept at making her feel that was happening, even when the opposite was true.

In fact the relationship between the Queen and Disraeli was far more interesting, significant, and historically important than that between her and John Brown, which has had so much attention focused on it. The six years between 1874 and 1880 restored her self-confidence and set the tone for the last two decades of her reign. There was a kind of love that flickered amid its complexities. She had a tender regard for his health and worried that he was not taking care of himself. Gladly she made him Earl of Beaconsfield 1876 so that he could exercise his office in the less demanding House of Lords. He wrote to Lady Bradford that 'I love the Queen – perhaps the only person in the world left to me that I do love.' And he laid his devotion at the Faery's feet. In a birthday message, he could say:

> 'Today Lord Beaconsfield ought fitly, perhaps, to congratulate a powerful Sovereign on her imperial sway, the vastness of her Empire, and the success and strength of her fleets and armies. But he cannot, his mind is in another mood. He can only think of the strangeness of his destiny that it has come to pass that he should be the servant of one so great, and whose infinite kindness, the brightness of whose intelligence and the firmness of whose will, have enabled him to undertake labours to which he would otherwise be quite unequal, and supported him in all things by a condescending sympathy, which in the hour of difficulty alike charms and inspires. Upon the Sovereign of many lands and many hearts may an omnipotent Providence shed every blessing that the wise can desire and the virtuous deserve!'

The Queen had no trouble in recognising herself in the mirror thus held up to her, and lived up to it. Though she would never relish the thought of public appearance, at her Vizier's adroit suggestion that it was for her glory and not for her duty, she would do it. He even, on occasion, got her to change her travel plans. When the Russian Tsar was visiting London in 1874, and she was due to leave for Balmoral two days before his departure, neither the Foreign Secretary nor the Prince of Wales could get her agreement to postpone her own journey. They were concerned that the Tsar would take it as an insult, but she saw no reason why the Queen of England's routine should be disrupted for a Russian Emperor. In the end Disraeli had to persuade her, and she did it 'for Mr Disraeli's sake'.

CHAPTER 5

The Making of an Empress

The sense of a British Empire had been gradually growing during Victoria's reign, as the motley range of British 'possessions' across the globe, from continent and semi-continents to tiny islands, gradually assumed the status of colonies and a Colonial Secretary was appointed to administer them in a general way. Governors or Governors-General were appointed, and they joined the dominions over which Victoria was Queen. She was never to visit any of them: Tuscany would be the furthest extent of her travels, though Bertie had visited Canada, and would visit India in 1876, and the nautical Affie had landed in South Africa and India. 'Empire' was simply a convenient way to describe all these territories in one, and the Queen was never an Empress in any formal, titular sense until 1876. Piece by piece through her years on the throne, by war, by treaty, by walking in and staking a claim, the British flag came to wave over more and more of the vast Indian sub-continent. The most populous and richest of her dominions, it was governed by a Viceroy – the only one apart from the Viceroy of Ireland – and a Secretary of State. India, or parts of it, had been an empire not so very long ago: even at the time of the Mutiny, in 1857, the last of the Mughal dynasty, Bahadur Shah II, had been hailed by the insurgents as an independent ruler, before dying in exile in Rangoon.

Empires were in vogue in Europe during the 1870s, and the national pretensions and ambitions they expressed were accompanied by a scramble to acquire colonies in other continents. Steamships, steam trains, and the rise of industry had created a hunger for raw materials and primary products of all kinds, together with the means to transport and distribute them. Colonies promised wealth as well as glory. Even a small-scale monarch, like Victoria's cousin, Leopold II, now King of the Belgians, could claim a huge territory, the Congo, in the heart of Africa. Only Russia, already the largest country on earth, and Austria-Hungary, sapped by war and internal dissensions, did not participate. Great Britain had a long head start in this race, but this did not stop it collecting new territories, especially in southern Africa. Within Britain, the two great political parties had differing views about the Empire. Gladstonian Liberals considered it as a responsibility, even a burden. While 'Retrenchment' was their cry, reflecting the old Whig concern to keep down taxes and government interference, it also offered a stick to the Tories. They accused the Liberals of neglecting the Navy, and of hazarding Britain's position in the world by penny-pinching policies. There was certainly a strong anti-war and anti-colonialist strain among the more radical members. The Liberals accused the Tories of 'Imperialism', by which they meant adventurism and arrogance in diplomacy and foreign affairs. The Tories, however, gloried in their own definition of Imperialism, which meant preserving, enlarging, and profiting from, the Empire. The years from 1874 confirmed Victoria's move away from the Whiggism of her early years as Queen, to a Disraelian Imperialist Toryism.

There was a price to pay for encouraging the Queen's self-confidence and sense of being the fount of national policy. The implicit trust, not to make impossible demands, was tested on several occasions. It was very much at the Queen's behest that the Public Worship Regulation Act of 1874 was passed, making it an offence to practise certain rituals in the Church of England service that were seen as excessively Catholic. Victoria, whose religious instincts were closer to Calvin than to Cranmer, felt there was a pro-Catholic trend that must be stopped: 'I am very nearly a Dissenter – or rather more a Presbyterian – in my feelings, so very Catholic do I think we are.' When the Act became law, a few Ritualist priests were prosecuted and briefly imprisoned during the years 1877–87. Disraeli did not have Gladstone's consuming interest in religious matters and without the Queen's powerful urging would have been most unlikely to introduce the Act. As it was, the appointment of senior clergy in the Church of England was one of the very few topics on which they disagreed; the Queen was still a supporter of the 'Broad Church' and her Prime Minister, more concerned to keep a balance and to appoint men who would be respected by their colleagues, was often obliged to defend appointments which she considered dangerously or offensively pro-Ritualist. Theological and liturgical controversies were no longer likely to shake a country in which people's lives were becoming increasingly secular and a scientific and social materialism was spreading. The Queen tapped a more modern strain with her angry objection to the practice of vivisection of animals, then becoming much more common as doctors and scientists searched deeper into human physiology, the sources of disease, and the effects of drugs and surgical techniques. Her detestation led directly to an Act of 1876 which, if it did not prohibit vivisection, at least regulated it and established conditions for the practice. She had always had, and loved, dogs and dogs were the principal victims of the vivisectors. Few of the Queen's ideas were modern, however. Her attitude to modern inventions was cool. Improvements made by the railway companies to her royal trains were not always appreciated. When her train was among the first to have vestibule connections, linking her day coach and sleeping coach, she would only use it when the train was brought to a halt. When the London & North Western Company, intending a pleasant surprise, installed electric lighting, she demanded that the old oil lamps be reinstalled.

The new confidence she felt with Disraeli's premiership, and Disraeli's expressed desire to accommodate her wishes, prompted the Queen to raise a matter that she had cherished for a long time, ever since the final deposition of the Mughal Emperor in Delhi in 1858. As she grew older, and spent longer on the throne, she became ever more conscious of her status as 'the doyenne of Sovereigns'. Around her, she had seen empires rise and fall. Napoleon III had died in exile in England and France was again, and definitively, a republic. Napoleon's widow, Eugénie, was still given full imperial honours in England,

and some suggested that she outranked the reigning Queen. Prussia, a minor state when she had become Queen, now was the centre of an empire, and Victoria had been affronted at the thought that her son-in-law Fritz, heir to an upstart emperor, might outrank her son, the Prince of Wales. In 1867, there had occurred the colonialist disaster in which Maximilian, brother of the Austrian Emperor Franz Josef, had been briefly installed as Emperor of Mexico, with French support, before being defeated and shot dead by Mexican nationalists.

There was no fear of any such successful uprising in British India. It was in India that Victoria saw the possibility of imperial recognition and distinction that would underscore her position as undisputed senior monarch among the kings and queens of the world. She broached the topic with Disraeli only to find that while he, of course, agreed that the title was both legitimate and deserved, he was by no means sure that the time was right or that Parliament would approve. However, almost every aspect of his foreign policy seemed to tend towards the East. In 1875, overruling Cabinet opposition and without consulting Parliament (pleading haste), he had organised the British purchase of a controlling interest in the Suez Canal from the Khedive of Egypt. Rothschilds had made an instant loan of £4,000,000 to conclude the deal, which snatched the Canal from under the noses of the French. The Queen had been kept informed and, when the deed was done, was told the canal was hers: 'It is just settled: you have it, Madam .... Four millions sterling! And almost immediately ... the entire interest of the Khedive is now yours, Madam.' He duly reported that 'the Faery is in ecstasies.' The grandiose nature of such a scheme, and the almost impudent ease with which Disraeli carried it off, inflamed the Queen's ambition. Surely the way to an imperial title was now open?

In the spring of 1876, the government brought forward a Bill to alter the Queen's title of Queen of the United Kingdom of Great Britain and Ireland to include that of Empress of India. It was to be hereditary: Bertie would become an emperor. Victoria, if not Disraeli, was surprised by the extent of opposition.

William Ewart Gladstone, from outside Parliament, was among the most vociferous objectors, but many within Parliament were against the change. Liberals disliked and feared the imperialist pretensions of the title. Many on the Tory side felt that the title of Queen of England was not something that could be improved on, and that the honour of the Crown was diminished by its juxtaposition with the gewgaws of an oriental potentate. One hundred and thirty members of the Commons opposed the Bill, but the imperialists had their way. Victoria had to wait until 1 January 1877 for her new status to take effect, and on that day she gave a great banquet in Windsor Castle, at which the black dress was emblazoned with diamonds and other jewels, gifts from the Rajahs, Nizams, Akunds, and other sub-monarchs of the Empire of India. The toast, 'To the Queen-Empress', was given by Prince Arthur. From then on, her signature was Victoria RI – Regina et Imperatrix.

The resourceful Disraeli found a job for the Marquess of Lorne, still awaiting his time to inherit the dukedom and with nothing much to do. With Louise, he went off to the new capital of Ottawa as Governor-General of Canada in 1878. That year Arthur married a Prussian princess, Louise, a cousin of his brother-in-law Fritz, but this did little to warm the chilly relations between the Berlin court and that of London. The elderly Emperor William I was very much under the dominance of his Chancellor, Bismarck; and Bismarck wanted to keep Great Britain on the outer periphery of European affairs. Arthur, whom his mother had created Duke of Connaught in 1874, was established in his military career, and, unlike Bertie, showed signs of proficiency as a field commander. He had always been Victoria's favourite among her sons, perhaps because he was the most biddable. Leopold remained a focus of anxiety for her because of his haemophilia. His delicacy and uncertain health, and perhaps a Hanoverian temper, made him far from biddable. He was able to get away with a degree of disobedience which filled his siblings with some awe. Aged twenty-five in 1878, he announced that he found Balmoral intolerable (something that others inside and outside the family had often felt but never dared express). Ignoring her wish, he went off for a week in Paris instead of accompanying her to Scotland. He ultimately joined up with the family party, but not before his mother's rage had exploded, as if he had committed high treason. He had attempted to subvert 'the authority of the Sovereign and the Throne'. Nowhere was she more imperious than in her dealings with her own family: here at least the constitutional queen was determined to be an absolute monarch. Her spats with Leopold always abated, however. He was invaluable to her as an honorary private secretary, especially as their views on most matters converged, but she also felt obliged to keep an eye on him, convinced that he was damaging his health and ignoring his doctors' advice.

Death was never long a stranger in large nineteenth-century families. The Queen's daughters, Vicky and Alice, each lost a son at a very young age. But in late 1878, the Hesse-Darmstadt family was ravaged by diphtheria. Alice lost a daughter and another son to it, before she herself contracted the disease. On the fateful date of 14 December she died. 'Dear Papa' were said to have been her final words. Victoria's relations with Alice had seesawed in the previous years – the mother had felt the daughter to be on occasions bossy, scheming, and interfering. Alice had several times been reduced to asking her mother for money, and Victoria was always more prepared to dispense advice than cash. Now Alice was dead, aged only 35, after heroically nursing her contagiously ill children, and the Queen experienced a storm of grief. 'My precious child who stood by me and upheld me seventeen years ago on the same day taken, and by such an awful, fearful disease,' she wrote to Vicky. 'She had darling Papa's nature, and much of his self-sacrificing character and fearless and entire devotion to duty.' Alice had now entered the realm of those who in Victoria's eyes could do, or had done, no wrong. Three months later, Vicky's adored youngest son Waldemar died, also of diphtheria.

In 1879, Victoria turned sixty. By now she was indeed

a matriarch, to her subjects almost as much as to her widely extended family. She had been Queen for more than forty years – already the great majority of Britons could not remember a time when she had not been their head of state. In the past few years, public opinion had veered in her favour, prompted by her more frequent appearances and increasing venerability. During her reign, the overall prosperity of the country had increased dramatically. The market value of British exports quadrupled between 1842 and 1870, at which time it was more than three times greater than the foreign trade of the United States. The tonnage of ships entering British ports had more than doubled in the same period. The national income, reckoned at £532,000,000 in 1851, had almost doubled thirty years later. Mechanisation and improved distribution, with cheap imports of raw materials, ensured generally falling prices until the mid-1890s. Colossal fortunes were still being made, enlarged, and occasionally lost, and between rich and poor the gulf of experience and expectation was far deeper and more difficult to cross than it is today. But a modest rising trend in wages continued, with the great exception of agriculture, which was suffering both from lower prices and from new and heavy competition from American wheat and Australian lamb and wool. The incomes of farmers and landowners fell, and the farm workers suffered correspondingly. It was a time when a family could occupy a substantial house, with a couple of domestic servants, on an income of £300 a year, less than one per cent of what Parliament annually granted to the Queen; and when £1000 a year enabled a family to live in some style. A sense of national prosperity bred a degree of complacency. The country was not only rich but stable, not only stable but strong: the 'fleets and armies' Disraeli had evoked in his birthday message were disposed across the globe; not only strong but benevolent, for the aim of these forces was to preserve the pax Britannica, not in an arrogant or overbearing spirit but to contain the ambitions of other powers and preserve the peace of the world. Even at the time, many people inside and outside Victoria's realms challenged the assumptions and attitudes underlying this sense of Britain's imperial mission and destiny. Queen Victoria was not among them; she relished the idea of British supremacy, and with the ardently imperialist Disraeli as her Prime Minister, expected to see that supremacy exercised.

A challenge to this self-appointed role among the nations had begun in 1876, when Russian hostility to the Ottoman Empire became an open threat. The Ottoman Empire itself, once united and formidable, had become weak, with its many different nationalities and racial and religious groups seeking the right of independence and self-expression. There was already warfare going on among the Balkan states. The situation was highly confused; in some cases uprisings could be seen as legitimate struggles for national liberation (at least in the eyes of British Liberals and Radicals), others were battles between rival warlords of no democratic credentials; others were savage struggles between Christian and Muslim communities that had long coexisted under the Ottomans. The Sultan was seen as effete and powerless; his economy had been officially declared bankrupt in 1875. To Tsar Alexander, Turkey was 'the sick man of Europe' and should be dismembered. With the rulers of Austria and Germany, he had formed the Dreikaiserbund, the League of Three Emperors, an alliance born out of mutual suspicions, fears and rivalries, but which found a common purpose for a time in agreeing that Turkish weakness should be exploited. This in London became 'the Eastern Question' and was regarded with great seriousness. Disraeli took a strategic view – if Russia should push down through Bulgaria and seize Constantinople, then it would control the Dardanelles and exercise a direct threat on Britain's route to India and the Far East, via the Suez Canal. It was therefore necessary to support Turkey.

In April 1877, Russia declared war on Turkey. The Empress of India identified herself closely with Disraeli's view. She had always been suspicious of Russia and now urged him to use the country's fleets and armies to keep the Tsar and his forces in check. The Foreign Secretary, Lord Derby, son of the former premier, was sufficiently worried to write to Disraeli expressing concern: 'Is there not just a risk of encouraging her in too large ideas of her personal power, and too great indifference to what the public expects? I only ask; it is for you to judge.' Much of British public opinion was with her; it was the time of the 'Great Macdermott's' famous music-hall war song:

> 'We don't want to fight, but, by Jingo, if we do,
> We've got the ships, we've got the men, we've got the money too.
> We've fought the Bear before, and while Britons shall be true,
> The Russians shall not have Constantinople.'

But much of British public opinion was not of the same opinion. The news of massacres of Christians in the Balkans – the 'Bulgarian Atrocities' – had brought William Gladstone forcefully back into political life. In a succession of huge public meetings he stormed against Disraeli's and Victoria's pro-Turkish policy. Even within the Cabinet, the Foreign Secretary and Secretary for India were urging caution. Examination of military strength and requirements showed that Britain did after all not have enough men to mount a war against Russia. The Queen, in a crescendo of martial fervour, several times threatened abdication: 'If England is to kiss Russia's feet, she will not be a party to the humiliation of England and would lay down her crown,' she wrote to Disraeli. The government sent a British fleet as far as Gallipoli, but merely as a gesture. With Bismarck playing the part of peacemaker, a peace treaty was signed between Turkey and Russia in March 1878, and the Congress of Berlin that summer attempted to re-establish the stability of Eastern Europe. Disraeli played an important part in moderating the heavy demands of Russia, and was the star of the Congress. The Queen was delighted. She had viewed Gladstone's campaign with indignation, and his return to Parliament with concern. In her view he was half-mad;

his overwhelming moral fervour was something she could neither understand nor admire.

Against the background of colonial warfare in Afghanistan and South Africa, the pro- and anti-imperialist arguments raged for another two years. The Zulu War against Cetewayo's people, launched by the British, was to strike home directly at the royal family. The heir to Napoleon III of France, honoured in Britain by his title of Prince Imperial, had been living in exile with his mother at Camden Place, Chislehurst. He attended the Military Academy at Woolwich and, keen to see war at first hand, pleaded to be allowed to join the army in South Africa. Aged twenty-three, he was killed when a scouting party was taken by surprise; his horse had bolted and his British escorts shamefully fled. The Queen, at Balmoral, broke with her rigid routine by coming south to condole with the Empress Eugénie. The last of the Bonapartes was accorded a full state funeral with all the panoply Great Britain could muster.

With misplaced confidence in the public's verdict, the government called an early general election at the end of March 1880. The result of 1874 was reversed and the Liberals returned with a very large majority. The Queen was deeply upset, not merely by the defeat of Disraeli, but by the fact that Gladstone was clearly the dominant figure in the Liberal Party. To Disraeli, who accepted the result with philosophy and dignity, she wrote that the defeat was a great public misfortune and that she was deeply grieved at having to part with 'the kindest and most devoted as well as one of the wisest Ministers the Queen has ever had.' His reply was equally deeply felt, and she went on take an exceptional step for one who took her position with such solemn seriousness: their continuing correspondence should move to the familiar first person, which she otherwise only used with her own family:

> When we correspond – which I hope we shall on
> many a *private* subject and without anyone being

astonished or offended, and even more without anyone knowing about it – I hope it will be in this more easy form. You can be of such use to me about my family and other things and about great public questions.

Her Private Secretary, Sir Henry Ponsonby, himself a Liberal, gave her the unpalatable advice that Gladstone had to be invited to form the government, and tried to assure her that the 'Grand Old Man' of the Liberals was both loyal and devoted to her. This was true, but Victoria would have none of it. The resounding attacks on Disraeli and the imperialist policy struck her as nothing short of treachery. In terms vehement even for her, she wrote:

'She would sooner *abdicate* than send for or have any *communication* with that *half-mad* firebrand ... others but herself *may submit* to his democratic rule, but *not the* Queen.'

She sought Disraeli's advice and he recommended Lord Hartington, who had led the Liberals during Gladstone's years of retirement. But neither 'Harty-Tarty', nor Lord Granville, known to the political world as 'Pussy', nor any other Liberal grandee, could form a government that did not have Mr Gladstone in it; and for his part, the only government he was interested in was one led by himself. There was no alternative, and the Queen did not abdicate. She sent for Mr Gladstone and, in her chilliest manner, requested him to form her government. Once again the frigid and impersonal audiences were resumed, intensified by the fact that she was opposed to much of what he proposed to do. She had opened Parliament on three occasions for Disraeli; she had only done it once for Gladstone, in 1871, and then it was for her own motive. At least, however, she now allowed her Prime Minister to sit during their private audiences; until Disraeli's latter years, etiquette had always required them to stand. Strachey recorded:

'When Lord Derby, the Prime Minister, had an
audience of Her Majesty after a serious illness, he
mentioned it afterwards, as a proof of the royal favour,
that the Queen had remarked, "How sorry she was she
could not ask him to be seated." '

The ex-Vizier, now Leader of Her Majesty's Loyal Opposition, was not to survive very long. On 19 April 1881, Lord Beaconsfield died, aged seventy-five, after a bronchial chill. The Queen had followed his illness with anxious concern, sending him primroses and messages.

'I send some Osborne primroses, and I meant to pay you
a little visit this week but I thought it better you should
be quite quiet and not speak. And I beg you will be very
good and obey the doctors and commit no imprudence.'

She would have accorded him a grand funeral and a tomb in Westminster Abbey, but his own instructions were for burial in Hughenden Churchyard by the side of his wife, and she contented herself with a memorial tablet in the church there. His death was a great loss to her, both emotionally and politically; she at first described it as 'overwhelming' to Lord Salisbury, who followed Disraeli as Conservative leader in the House of Lords:

'... this dreadful loss, irreparable to the country and
Europe, to his many friends, and above all to herself!
His devotion, unselfishness and kindness she can *never,
never*, forget; her gratitude is everlasting.'

Once again she was on her own, alone on the pinnacle, but she did not collapse in on herself, or seek a new seclusion. The Disraeli years had brought her back to a confidence which did not now desert her. 'Her Majesty's Government' would find that, for all its popular mandate, it had an unrelenting one-woman Opposition.

Partial re-emergence into public view and public life, combined with her determination to supervise the government closely, made the Queen quite busy in the 1880s, though there were still prolonged periods at Balmoral and Osborne. Her large family (she would end up by having forty-two grandchildren and eighty-seven great-grandchildren) made its own demands on her time and sense of duty. At her command they visited frequently, and she wrote innumerable letters to those within the family circle and to acquaintances beyond. It is doubtful whether she had any friends in the normal sense of the word. Perhaps the only one had been Harriet, Duchess of Sutherland, her first Mistress of the Robes, but she, thirteen years older than Victoria, had died in 1868. She had a devoted group of ladies-in-waiting and maids of honour, who accompanied her for walks and drives, read to her, gave her news of the life of the 'Higher Classes', of whose antics she still sternly disapproved, and suffered the open windows and blasts of cold air that were inseparable from life with the Queen. They were companions, but not friends to whom she could open her heart. At a closer, family level, she still had Beatrice and Leopold as part of her immediate entourage. In 1880, Beatrice was twenty-three. Her eldest sister had been married six years and had had several children by that age, as had her mother. But if Victoria had her way, Beatrice was never going to marry at all. The youngest princess had long been selected as her mother's companion and helper in old age – a role which marriage would at best hinder and at worst make impossible. The Queen set out quite deliberately to make Beatrice seem and feel a child for as long as possible; her pet name was 'Baby'. When she was quite grown up, any reference to marriage or weddings at the dinner table when Princess Beatrice was present were immediately cut off, and the subject changed. Nothing was to give 'Baby' unsuitable ideas. For some years Beatrice accepted her part loyally. At least the Queen was no longer sunk in what had once seemed perpetual mourning. Even another attempt on her life, by one Roderick Maclean, did not daunt her. This attack, at

Windsor Station on 2 March 1882, was made with a loaded gun, but the weapon was struck upwards by an alert bystander. The gunman had earlier sent a poem to the Queen, which had been returned by a lady-in-waiting, 'The Queen never accepts manuscript poetry.' He was judged not guilty on grounds of insanity. Victoria enjoyed a wave of sympathy, noting that 'It is worth being shot at – to see how much one is loved.' There were outings, parties, and jollifications. Once again, she danced – at an Osborne party on the eve of Beatrice's twenty-first birthday, she recorded that 'I danced a Quadrille and a valse, which I had not done for eighteen years, and I found I could do it as well as ever.' She had taken to foreign travel: not pilgrimages to Coburg, but month-long stays in new and relaxing places, the Italian Lakes, the French Riviera. She visited republican Paris and met the French President. For those in attendance on her person, life became more interesting and varied. But her wish and expectation to have Leopold and Beatrice by her always were to be disappointed.

Leopold, as her Private Secretary, was permitted access to the royal despatch boxes and state papers, something Disraeli had encouraged, though remarkable in that his eldest brother, the Prince of Wales, had no such privilege. But Leopold, Victoria and Disraeli thought alike, and Bertie's views were often different. Nor was Bertie felt to have much discretion. When Leopold announced his desire to marry, the Queen reluctantly acquiesced, and found him a bride as intelligent as he was, Princess Helena of Waldeck-Pyrmont, a veritable bluestocking among Germanic princesses. They were married at Windsor in 1882. On 28 April 1884, Leopold died suddenly in his sleep of a cranial haemorrhage, leaving a daughter and an unborn son. The second of her children to die before her, he left the Queen feeling 'utterly crushed … . How dear he was to me, how I watched over him!' But she was able to spare a thought for 'that poor loving young wife'. That same year, Beatrice fell in love with Prince Henry of Battenberg whom she had met at the wedding of her cousin Victoria in Darmstadt.

At the thought of losing the second of the selected companions who would see her through her declining years, the Queen was furious. The demanding and implacable aspect of her character linked with endless self-pity and expressed in vehement rage, came to the fore. For several months she would scarcely speak to Beatrice. She refused to consent to the marriage and her agreement was only obtained after Henry had agreed to reside in England. Then she accepted the situation and settled down to like her latest son-in-law, having ensured that 'she, sweet child, remains with poor, old, shattered me.' Always a person of moods and swings of temper, she was probably the only person in the country who would have described herself in such terms. To her family she was all too evidently capable of asserting herself and insisting that her will be done, whatever the effect on other people's lives.

And yet she had suffered a grievous loss in 1883 – one that affected her personally and directly. In March of that year, her Highland Servant, John Brown, died, at the age of 57. He had been suffering from erysipelas, not a life-threatening condition, but his system had also been weakened by alcoholism. Brown had been in her service since 1851, and several other members of his family were also employed at Balmoral, where Victoria's regard for the local population encouraged a spirit of service that was intensely loyal but also far less deferential than the normal attitude expected by the English nobility from their domestic staff. It was more akin to the traditional bond between a chieftain and his clansfolk: a bond already much eroded and virtually anachronistic elsewhere in the Highlands. John Brown's agility, strength and alertness as a ghillie (an outdoor servant who helped in deerstalking, fishing, and outside activities generally) had caught the eye of the Prince Consort, and it was Albert who selected Brown to lead the Queen's pony on their mountain expeditions. Other Highlanders, like her personal piper, William Ross, also enjoyed her favour, but in Brown Victoria saw all the virtues she admired among the Highlanders combined in one person.

The relationship between the Queen and the ghillie was a subject of curious and often prurient speculation almost as soon as it became known outside the royal circle. During her period of seclusion and unpopularity, sneering references were often made to 'Mrs Brown' and it was widely rumoured that she was receiving sexual consolation from the virile and unmarried Scot. From his arrival at Osborne in 1864, Brown was a permanent fixture in her household, both indoors and out, at home and abroad (where his kilt aroused curiosity and admiration). Among its other members, even her own children, there were sometimes conflicts of loyalty, differences of opinion with her, causes for argument and reproof, but Brown was wholly and always on her side. His virtues were his devotion and dedication to her, his discretion, and his instinctive understanding of her needs and moods. Total loyalty on his side was repaid by the Queen in the same coin. Anyone who ventured a criticism of Brown in her presence was walking on the thinnest of ice. His patrols of the shrubberies in search of Fenian terrorists were perhaps overdone, but he would have given his life for her, and she knew it. It was his hand that had thrust down Fergus O'Connor, and his hand more than once that had stayed an over-excited horse that threatened to run away with her. His presence gave her a sense of physical security, but the feeling went deeper than that. In times of grief, she treasured his 'strong, kind, simple words' and at other times she relished his pithy conversation and sharp observation of the scene around him, so different to the decorous, conventional, and formal remarks of others. Though a man of fine presence on state occasions, Brown was quite impervious to the everyday protocol and procedures of royal life, and his brusqueness in passing on his mistress's messages and wishes became notorious, and was not appreciated by persons of dignity and high position. Brown did not need to care – he often treated the Queen in the same way. No other man in her life would, or could, have addressed her as 'Woman'. But, as with Disraeli, it was the woman in the Queen who responded to this (very different) approach. In allowing, and enjoying, such familiarity, Victoria felt no threat to her regal status. Lytton Strachey's subtle pen suggests how this could be:

> '... after all, it is no uncommon thing for an autocratic dowager to allow some trusted indispensable servant to adopt towards her an attitude of authority which is jealously forbidden to family or friends: the power of a dependent still remains, by a psychological sleight-of-hand, one's own power, even when it is exercised over oneself. When Victoria meekly obeyed the commands of her henchman to get off her pony or put on her shawl, was she not displaying, and in the highest degree, the force of her volition?'

After Albert's death, she had vowed to make herself dependent on no man, but this was different; John Brown had no wish to make himself a power behind the throne and his gruff attentions were focused on her safety, comfort, and peace of mind – and no more, apart from keeping the other Highland domestics, who gradually spread south from Balmoral, firmly under his thumb. Frederick Ponsonby, son of her Private Secretary, wrote in *Recollections of Three Reigns*:

> '... whether there was any quite unconscious sexual feeling in the Queen's regard for her faithful servant I am unable to say, but ... I am quite convinced that if such a feeling did exist, it was quite unconscious on both sides, and that their relations up to the last were simply those of employer and devoted retainer.'

For a man of Brown's stamp, it was not altogether a natural form of existence and the stresses of court life, and the isolation of his role, encouraged his dependence on whisky. Victoria perhaps appreciated the self-sacrificial aspect of his life in turning a blind eye to this, and in such unusual concessions as allowing him to smoke in her presence: something that was not permitted to princes. He was paid £400 a year, a substantial salary, and, with free accommodation, and taking no holidays, had little to spend it on. He gave generously to many causes. With the ending of such a relationship, at Brown's relatively early age, the Queen was of course deeply distraught. In 1877, she had sent him a Christmas card, inscribed, 'To my best friend, J.B. From his best friend. V.R.I.' For her, his death was an irreparable loss. To Vicky she wrote that ' ... all is gone in this world, and all seems unhinged again in thousands of ways.' The deprivation of his presence was sharpened by the fact that she had recently slipped, fallen, and injured her leg, making walking difficult: how much that absent strong arm would have been appreciated. It was from then on that she took to using a walking stick.

The publication in 1884 of *More Leaves from the Journal of Our Life in the Highlands* was partly intended as an explicit tribute to John Brown's memory. It was dedicated to 'My Loyal Highlanders and especially to the memory of my devoted personal attendant and faithful friend JOHN BROWN', and it ended with a further encomium:

> 'His loss to me (ill and helpless as I was at the time from an accident) is irreparable, for he deservedly possessed my entire confidence; and to say that he is daily, nay, hourly, missed by me, whose lifelong gratitude he won by his constant care, attention, and devotion, is but a feeble expression of the truth.'

Such unburdening of her heart – in the first person – to her subjects shows how much at one Victoria now felt with her people; or perhaps how much she felt they were at one with her. Gone were the days of mistrust on her part and cynicism and reproach on theirs (a few unrepentant old-style Radicals and new-style Socialists, and anti-monarchist groups of anarchists excepted). Her confidences were regarded with alarm by her family and senior courtiers, who felt that her sentiments exposed her to public misunderstanding and ridicule, and reduced the proper mystique of the Crown and its distance from the populace. The court was vicariously embarrassed on her behalf, but she was sublimely untroubled by their scruples, and only distressed by her children's refusal to properly appreciate the book. The Prince of Wales pleaded with her, in vain, to print it for private circulation only. He regarded it as 'an act of insanity'. Like its predecessor, it was an instant international bestseller, and among the great majority of readers it increased sympathy with, and affection for, its author.

However, the Queen's advisers did win a battle over another planned publication. She had written a more extensive personal memoir of Brown and his years of service to her. Randall Davidson, the new Dean of Windsor (later Archbishop of Canterbury), risked her anger and displeasure by persisting in his advice not to publish this, even offering to resign if she thought he was abusing his position. In the end, she took his advice, and the manuscript was put aside. Almost certainly it was burned by Princess Beatrice after the Queen's death, along with much of the diaries. It is likely that a snobbish horror at the very notion of the Queen writing the life of a lower-class servant, as much as the urge to prevent further disclosure of her personal feelings, prompted the Dean to imperil his career in order to save his sovereign from herself.

The successive events within her household, glad or traumatic, did not divert Victoria from keeping an eye on what her government was up to. She considered some of its members to be dangerously radical and was not convinced that Gladstone could, or even wanted to, control them. The government was not as strong as its majority suggested, suffering from growing tensions between the old Whig views – which in most ways were conservative and certainly considered too much legislation a bad thing – and the new radical views, which saw Parliament as the engine for social reform and wanted ever more legislation to bring it about. Gladstone's genuine desire to maintain an ethical foreign policy was ill-suited to the imperialist temper of the times, at home and abroad; and his distaste for colonial possessions, and the problems they presented, had to struggle with the awareness that Britain had a colonial Empire, whether he liked it or not, and it required administration, policing, and protection. As a result of these tensions, his second long term of office did not achieve the same pace of reform as his first had done. Gladstone also began to be preoccupied by the state of affairs in Ireland. A new political leader, Charles Stuart Parnell, had formed the majority of the one hundred Irish MPs into a disciplined bloc with an insistent Home Rule policy. In Ireland itself, there was intense and often violent social unrest against the economic dominance of the English and Anglo-Irish who owned most of the land and whose (mostly) Unionist politics and Anglican religion made them appear more like a colonial governing class than an integral part of a national community. Gladstone's acceptance of the principle of self-government in Ireland was of a piece with his support of national independence and self-government for all countries. But his Irish policy was not shared by any of his Whig, and some of his Radical, associates. Nor was it shared by the Queen.

Victoria had been crowned Queen of the United Kingdom of Great Britain and Ireland – that was her realm, the unified core and basis of her sovereignty, with which she absolutely identified herself, and she was deeply suspicious of any tampering with it. She had never interested herself much in Ireland, even during the terrible time of the Great Famine of the late 1840s. She had seen agitation for Irish self-government rise and fall before, in the days of O'Connell, and did not see why it should be encouraged now. Mr Gladstone had already disestablished the Anglican Church in Ireland: now that Ireland again had a Roman Catholic hierarchy in place, what more might happen? For many members of the Commons, and even more of the Lords, the commanding issue was a threat to property. A devolved government in Dublin, elected by popular suffrage, would be hostile to landowners; it might even dispossess them.

It would certainly restrict their powers and control their rents; and the rot might spread to England. The murder in Dublin of the new Chief Secretary for Ireland, Lord Frederick Cavendish and the Under-Secretary, Charles Burke, in April 1882, confirmed the worst fears of those who believed the only answer for Ireland was heavy repression: a view with which Victoria fully agreed. Once again the scene was set for an Irish wind to cause a catastrophic storm in British political life.

Meanwhile, in a way that would have tickled Disraeli, the Queen had found a domestic stick to beat the government with. In 1883, she wrote to Gladstone to express her concern about the housing of the poor. This was scarcely a new topic; it had been a cry of reformers for more than thirty years, and Victoria's discovery of it came rather late, but nevertheless she asserted its urgency ('involving the very existence of thousands – nay millions') and pressed for action. In 1884, a Royal Commission on working-class housing was set up by the government, with the Prince of Wales as a member. Bertie took his role sufficiently seriously to speak forcefully in the House of Lords for remedial action. This won the approval of the Queen. By now she and he had established a kind of modus vivendi, in which she did not inquire too closely into his life; she had long since given up trying to rule it. Bertie was not going to change his spots. Lytton Strachey passes on a story of the Prince of Wales arriving 'blamelessly' late for a dinner at Osborne around this time, and being so unnerved by the thought of the Queen's displeasure that he hid behind a pillar. Strachey ascribes it to fear of the Queen, but his behaviour is unlikely to have been because of his mother: perhaps his own almost manic obsession with punctuality (which he shared with her) was to blame. In many ways his and her views concurred, both being ardent imperialists with a Liberal tinge in domestic policy, and their meetings were generally cordial. On 9 November 1883, she recorded in her diary, 'Dear Bertie's 42nd birthday. May God bless him and long preserve him for the good of his country! Warm-hearted, kind and amiable, he is always a very good son to me.' Although this was faint praise compared with her comments on Albert's qualities, it shows a motherly appreciation of the Prince's best aspects. The only occasions on which she lost her temper with him were when he suggested it might be her duty to do something which she did not want to do. But he was not alone in this respect: the only three men who could do this with any success were by then all dead.

In her concern for the urban poor, Victoria was showing one of the few last vestiges of the social concerns that the Prince Consort had taught her. Her political views and social attitudes were becoming ever more firmly conservative. She always considered herself a Liberal, and claimed that it was they who had changed, not her. There was some truth in this, but it was rather that while political ideas had moved on, in concert with social change, the Queen's had remained fixed at around 1841. Though never as partisan as she had been in her first months as Queen, there was by 1880 no doubt in anyone's mind, including Victoria's own, that by now her sympathies lay firmly with the Conservatives. Her acceptance of modern inventions was tepid: the most-often quoted example, her use of chloroform, was prompted by her great aversion to the 'animal' aspects of childbirth. Her resistance to innovation was often determined. She complained voluminously about those of her daughters and daughters-in-law who saw fit to breast-feed their own babies – she herself had gladly passed that task on to wet-nurses. Always seeing herself as a woman placed by Divine and inscrutable Providence in a situation that was properly a man's, she did not see herself in any way as a beacon for female emancipation. She had no time for those who wanted to give women the vote or right of entry to universities, and detested the leaders of such campaigns. When her daughters, notably Vicky and Alice, identified themselves with women's causes, she became angry. She once wrote to Gladstone, expressing 'the strongest aversion for the so-called and most erroneous Rights of Women' (one of the few topics upon which they could agree). She told Sir Theodore Martin that the subject 'makes the Queen so furious that she cannot contain herself', and expressed a view that one prominent aristocratic lady, a vigorous campaigner for women's rights, ought to get 'a good whipping'. In this attitude, as in many others, the Queen was not wholly consistent. Certain women who stood against the tide of events won her admiration and support. Florence Nightingale was the prime example. But Florence Nightingale had dedicated herself to a field of activity that was entirely compatible with femininity. Had she challenged male supremacy in some other area, by seeking to become a doctor, for example, Victoria would have been less impressed.

Gladstone's reluctance to embrace Britain's imperial role was greatly resented by the Queen. Since their personal meetings were no more frequent than they had to be, missives sped to and fro, with royal expostulations and lengthy Prime Ministerial explanations. As Gladstone had foreseen at the time, possession of the Suez Canal was not an unmitigated blessing to Britain. It demanded British involvement in Egypt, and that in turn demanded British involvement in the Sudan, previously dominated by Egypt, where a religious leader, Mohammed Ahmed (Muhammad Ahmad), known as 'the Mahdi' or 'expected one' began from 1881 to establish his own rule over large areas. By the end of 1883, his success had left a number of British garrisons isolated, including that at Khartoum, the capital. A former governor of the Sudan, General Charles Gordon, was sent to the Sudan in February 1884 to report on the situation. Gladstone's instinct was for British withdrawal. Gordon, a thoroughgoing imperialist, chose to install himself at Khartoum and ask for reinforcements, in a deliberate attempt to force government action. The Mahdi's army besieged the town and for ten months Gordon and his small force held them off. His plight brought the simmering national mood of jingoism to fever pitch. An expedition to rescue Gordon and smash the Mahdi was demanded, with the Queen vociferously at the forefront. For months the government temporised. To Victoria the issue was simple –

British interests, British prestige, and British lives were under threat: what use were the fleets and armies unless mobilised to put matters to rights? To Gladstone, furious with Gordon and far more aware of the difficulties involved, quite apart from his moral objections to colonialism and colonial wars, the issue was far from simple. But he failed to convince the country. In August 1884, a relief expedition was assembled and sent on the long journey up the Nile, while an excited public speculated on whether it would be in time. The result was the worst possible. General Wolseley's relieving force reached Khartoum on 28 January 1885, to find that the insurgents had stormed it only two days before. Gordon had died fighting. When the news reached Britain, the Queen noted implacably in her journal that 'The Government is alone to blame, by refusing to send the expedition until it was too late.' To her the insubordinate and intransigent Gordon was 'innocent, noble, heroic' and his blood, and that of many others, was on Gladstone's hands. Telegraphic communication between her and the government was normally in code, but now she deliberately sent a message in plain English in the hope that her view would be widely published, ' ... to think that all this might have been prevented and many precious lives saved by earlier action is too frightful.' Such a direct public criticism of the government, had it reached the public domain, would itself have caused a serious political crisis, and Victoria was undoubtedly emboldened by the feeling that she spoke for public opinion. In fact, the telegram was not leaked, and a confrontation was averted, though Gladstone told his friend and biographer, John Morley, that he would 'never set foot in Windsor again.'

Victoria was meanwhile writing directly to General Wolseley, asking him not to contemplate a retreat from Khartoum, and expressing her fear that ' ... some of the Government are very unpatriotic and do not feel what is a necessity.' She asked him to destroy the letter, knowing well that she was pushing her constitutional role beyond the accepted limits. In the strength of her feeling, she even wrote to the General's wife:

> '*In strict confidence* I *must* tell you I think the Government are *more incorrigible* than ever, and I do think your husband should hold *strong* language to them, and *even* THREATEN to resign if he does not receive strong support and liberty of action ... Pray either destroy this, or lock it up ... .'

Wolseley, however, took his orders neither from the Queen nor his wife, but from the Secretary of State for War, and to Victoria's outrage, the British Army departed from the Sudan, leaving the Mahdi unconquered and Gordon unavenged.

The icy relations between the Queen and the government were clear when a Parnellian-Tory combination brought Parliamentary defeat to the Liberals in June 1885. Victoria was at Balmoral and declined to come back to London or Windsor; Gladstone did not see why he should have to go to Balmoral when it was the Queen's duty at such a time to be close to the seat of government. 'He seems to thinks I am just a machine to run up and down as he likes,' was her comment. In the end, she returned to London when it became clear that the Conservatives, under Lord Salisbury, were prepared to form a minority government (preparation of electoral rolls meant that a general election was not practicable until December). The thought of getting rid of Gladstone was well worth a few days away from Balmoral, even in the summer heat of Windsor. She offered him an earldom (though not the Order of the Garter, her personal accolade): he politely refused. Aged seventy-six, he was not yet ready to quit the House of Commons and the leadership of his party. A new cause had captured his moral zeal: after many years of opposing it, he had decided to support Home Rule for Ireland. He maintained his practice of making long speeches to huge public gatherings: this going beyond Parliament directly to the electorate, which earned him the by-name of 'the People's William', was deplored by the Queen. In October 1885, it drew from her a rare expression of irony, when she wrote to him:

'The Queen trusts Mr Gladstone is recovering from the hoarseness with which he has been troubled for so many months, and takes this opportunity of expressing a hope that he will spare himself from speaking at public meetings for some time to come.'

It was a vain hope. The Prince of Wales joined the Queen at the first Privy Council meeting with her new set of Conservative ministers. All seemed set for harmony and a hoped-for Tory victory at the election. The Queen, happy to have in Salisbury 'a minister in whom she could thoroughly confide', even opened the new session of Parliament (the last time she did so) specifically to show her support for his administration. But the Liberals won a majority of eighty-six over the Conservatives, and Parnell's Irish phalanx, also eighty-six strong, held the balance.

The year 1886 was to be a year of momentous events. In January, Salisbury resigned when Parnell again joined forces with Gladstone, and the Queen had to brace herself to receive the 'Grand Old Man' – whom she considered, as he knew, wild, fanatical, and reckless – as her Prime Minister once again. She had been writing to senior pro-Union Liberals like George Goschen to urge them to separate themselves from Gladstone, and she tried to get Goschen to lead a 'Loyalist' party. The introduction of Gladstone's first Home Rule Bill split his party, with ninety-three Liberals opposing it, including many of Gladstone's former ministers. The motion was lost by thirty votes. Gladstone took the issue to the country, but in the general election, the Conservatives won a majority of one hundred and fifteen and a few months later, Goschen became the first of numerous Liberal-Unionists to serve in a Conservative government, in his case as Chancellor of the Exchequer. Victoria might well feel relieved and triumphant. How far her open partisanship for the Tories, and her efforts to detach Gladstone's union-minded colleagues, played a part in the events of that year has often been argued over. The twentieth-century historian A J P Taylor considered Victoria a 'political null' before and after the time of the Prince Consort. Certainly there was nothing creative or original in her political views and stance, but it is impossible to believe that she counted for nothing at all. Reverence for the Crown was much more deeply ingrained among politicians then, and its influence was not negligible. Although she followed a large section of public opinion, rather than leading it, at the very least, knowledge of the Queen's ardently expressed views and desires helped to stiffen the resolve of those Liberals who were considering a rejection of their formidable leader's cherished and strongly argued policy. But two hundred and twenty-seven English, Welsh and Scottish MPs had voted for Gladstone's Bill, and the question of Irish Home Rule lay, like a hidden minefield, awaiting another day.

Salisbury resumed his ministry, and it was under the comfortable aegis of an aristocrat-led and imperialist-minded government that Victoria's fifty years on the throne were celebrated in 1887. Her health was generally good and her vitality was strong; the only real problem was a tendency to rheumatism, which had been present since her fall in March 1883. Perhaps her relish for cold fresh air and her indifference to damp, which had led to picnics in rain and even snow, were now catching up with her. A well-known French masseuse, Madame Charlotte Nautet, from the spa of Aix-les-Bains, made regular visits and became known in court circles as 'the Rubber', but her attentions had little effect. Victoria had always had a hearty appetite except when prostrated by grief, and it did not grow less in her later years. Overweight and not keen on exercise, she became increasingly stiff-jointed, and unable to walk for any distance. By now she had what she referred to as her 'rolling chair', a wheelchair in which she could be propelled along the corridors of great houses. This did not deter her from making numerous public appearances, however. The almost-royal receptions accorded to Gladstone in many towns, not least in Scotland (when Goschen lost his Edinburgh seat in 1866 she wrote, 'My dear Scotch behave like fools'), encouraged her to show her own popularity with her people. Jubilee celebrations took place all across the Empire and messages, tributes, and gifts poured in, from individuals as well as governments and rulers. The requests for her presence, the management of events, the reception and acknowledgement of all the gifts, took a great deal of management, and again Bertie proved his helpfulness in assisting with the plans and arrangements. The public reaction was mostly all that she could have wished. Only on one occasion was she disconcerted by 'a horrid noise'; when she opened the People's Palace in the East End of London on 14 May, a section of the crowd booed her – this was put down to Socialists and 'the worst Irish'. On 20 June, Victoria noted in her diary:

> 'The day has come and I am alone, though surrounded by many dear children ... 50 years today since I came to the Throne! God has mercifully sustained me through many great trials and sorrows.'

A great assemblage of European royalty came to join in the celebrations, including the Kings of Greece, Denmark, and the Belgians. She could rightly describe it as 'a large family dinner', for among the glittering assembly were very few who were not related to her by blood, marriage or very often both. She was greatly pleased by the presence of her senior son-in-law, Crown Prince Frederick of Germany. Fritz had been gravely ill with cancer of the throat, and his treatment was causing yet another in the long series of disputes and family crises between the British royal family and the Hohenzollerns. Vicky had called in a British specialist, who had counselled against a tracheotomy operation that German doctors had recommended. For a time under Dr Mackenzie's treatment the Prince's condition seemed to improve, and he rode behind Victoria's carriage, in white uniform, with eagled helmet and Field Marshal's baton, in the procession to Westminster Abbey on 21 June. His father's health was failing and it did not seem that it would be long before Frederick became German Emperor. The London crowd cheered him lustily, as they also did the more exotic royalties, the Indian maharajas, and other eastern kings and chiefs, whose peoples were now also subjects of the Queen-Empress, among them Queen Kapiolani of Hawaii.

Amid the splendours of the military and court uniforms, the central figure of Victoria in her open landau wore neither robe nor crown. The absence of regalia made her all the more conspicuous. Against all the advice of her daughters and close attendants, she wore her habitual black, a satin gown relieved by white and silver, with a bonnet decorated with white lace and diamonds – but a bonnet nonetheless. Of course every other lady involved in the ceremony had to have a bonnet too. There was a real sense of theatre achieved by this plainness of the little old lady in black, escorted by Indian cavalry and with all the gaudiness of high state ceremonial spread out before and behind her, which would not have been excelled by scarlet, ermine and gold. To Victoria, it simply emphasised what she was always at pains to remind importunate ministers and others, that she was a person, a lady, a widow. She might occupy a great position, but she was not going to subsume her own strong sense of self in the fancy dress that would make her into something impersonal and institutional. This simple piece of obstinacy made high drama out of what otherwise was mere spectacle, however splendid.

The widow of many years did not forget her husband on that day, and again she felt her solitude among many – 'I sat alone (oh! without my beloved husband, for whom this would have been such a proud day!).' Included in the music were Albert's Te Deum and his anthem Gotha. If the bugles, pipes, and drums sounded for her, they also sounded for the idea of Empire that she firmly associated herself with. The Indian cavalry escort, not the Household Cavalry, who were elsewhere in the great procession, were also a token of that. After the procession and service, there was an exhausting month of events of all kinds – parades, presentations, investitures, and receptions. Even when she removed to Osborne on 19 July, the Jubilee followed her, with a great review of the fleet at Spithead, and distinguished foreign visitors coming to take their leave. She was glad to make the retreat to Balmoral, though it had been a gratifying year as well as a tiring one. Beatrice, though pregnant, had been one of her main supports throughout the celebrations, and she gave birth to a daughter at Balmoral on 24 October. The child was christened at Crathie Church in a Church of Scotland service, though Victoria had no compunction, or apparent opposition, in inserting provision for godparents, something which was certainly not part of the Kirk's official ritual.

From the end of June 1887, two Indian servants were added to the troop of Scottish and English attendants, at first as waiters. Mohammed Buksh and Abdul Karim were both young men, aged twenty-four. Victoria enjoyed having them attend on her; Abdul Karim especially had an ingratiating charm and quite soon the Queen's Indian servants had a special status. Victoria's instructions to Major General Sir Thomas Denneby, Groom-in-Waiting, show her intense absorption in the detail of how the royal household should appear.

> 'Mohammed Buksh and Abdul Karim should wear in the *morning out of doors* at breakfast when they wait, their *new* dark blue dress and always at lunch with any 'Pageri' [turban] and sash *they like* only not the *Gold ones*. The Red dress and gold and white turban (or pageri) and sash to be *always worn at dinner in the evening*. If it is wet or cold the breakfast is *in doors* when they should always attend. As I often, *before* the days get too short take the tea out with me in the carriage, they might do some extra waiting instead, either *before* I go out, or when I come in. Better before I go out, stopping half an hour longer and should wait *upstairs* to answer a handbell. They should come in and out and bring boxes, letters, etc. *instead* of the *maids* ... .'

One wonders if the tea was still as once reported by John Brown, 'She don't much like tea – we tak oot biscuits and sperrits.'

After a time, Abdul Karim had made representations to the Queen that his status as a clerk made waiting at table an indignity. In 1889, he was formally appointed as the Queen's Munshi or clerk, becoming in effect her secretary for Indian matters. In the Queen's eyes the Munshi was a gentleman, by his own account of being the son of a doctor, but in any case entitled to that status by his position in her household. Her family and courtiers, who had been generally relieved by the death of John Brown six years before, were much less ready to accept him. 'Institutional racism' – a phrase non-existent at that time – was part of life in the British establishment. The only person who did not participate in it at all was the Queen. For the rest of her life she would fight a stout battle on Abdul Karim's behalf, against the prejudice and snobbery of the court. Though he never came to occupy a position like Brown's, he was given Brown's old room: a deliberate sign of special favour. In 1894, his status was raised to Queen's Indian Secretary and he was given the honorary distinguished title of Hafiz.

The court functionaries regarded him as an interloper, con man, and spy, passing state secrets to Afghanistan; they observed with suspicion the arrival of 'nephews' and 'wives' as the Munshi's own domestic establishment expanded. There were frequent attempts to impugn his character to the Queen, in the hope that she would let him go, but her loyalty was fully roused. When Frederick Ponsonby, son of her old Private Secretary, came back from India with evidence that Abdul Karim's father was no doctor, but a prison apothecary, it was Ponsonby she was furious with, not the Munshi. Secure in her own regality, class distinction made little difference to her. She was fond of reminding complainers that she had known two archbishops who were the sons of a butcher and a grocer respectively. Colour mattered to Victoria even less. To her, the Munshi personified that great eastern dominion of which she was Empress, and which had great allure for her. Under his tuition she learned some Hindustani and she was as happy to be photographed in his presence as she had been with John Brown. In 1897, the dispute became serious when she proposed to take Abdul Karim to France as part of her official entourage. The courtiers protested, sending the Queen into such a rage as she had not experienced for many years. She swept the contents of her desktop to the floor. It took the suavity and authority of Lord Salisbury, her Prime Minister, to mend matters. He explained that the French might not understand the Munshi's role, and that remarks and misunderstandings might arise to compromise the Queen's dignity. Abdul was left behind in England, but never behind in coming forward, he came along uninvited to join the royal party at Cimiez, to the consternation of the other members of the Queen's household. He remained her Indian Secretary until her death, after which he had to submit to most of his carefully preserved files and documents being burned at the order of King Edward VII. He removed to India, where Victoria had procured a property for him, Karim Lodge, and died in 1909.

Her Jubilee year set the tone for the final period of Queen Victoria's reign, which was to continue for longer than most people suspected. It was for her generally a mellow time, despite the upsets, excitements and minor intrigues of her court, some much-lamented deaths, and the uncertainties of royal existence for many of her European relations. For Great Britain, although the splendour and authority of Empire seemed undimmed, it was the time when both the United States and Germany overtook it in steel production, and the long lead gained by pioneering the rise of industry was lost with scarcely anyone noticing. The very fixity of the Queen's own person was a factor, albeit a minor one, in preventing the British from reassessing themselves: she seemed to confer a massive continuity on events. In Lytton Strachey's words, she was now 'a part of the establishment – an essential part as it seemed – a fixture – a magnificent, immovable sideboard in the huge saloon of state.'

The Queen was not so inanimate as that metaphor suggests. There were still tests for her to endure. In March 1888, on the death of his father, Frederick became German Emperor, and Vicky his Kaiserin. Victoria wrote to congratulate her eldest daughter.

> 'My OWN dear *Empress Victoria* it does seem an impossible dream, God bless her! You know *how* little I care for rank or Titles – but I cannot *deny* that *after* all that has been done & said, I am *thankful* and *proud* that dear Fritz and you should have come to the Throne.'

The professed disregard for rank or title is illustrative of how swings in Victoria's moods affected her view of events; this was the same Victoria who, on creating her son Leopold Duke of Albany, instructed that in her household he should continue to be known as 'Prince Leopold' – 'I always say no one can be a Prince, but any one can be a duke.' Unfortunately, despite the congratulations, it was all too clear that Fritz's time on the throne would be drastically short. Again struck down by cancer of the throat, he was mortally ill. Victoria, who had taken a holiday in Florence, returned by way of Germany to visit her son-in-law. All the susceptibilities of anti-British Prussianism (in which Fritz and Vicky's eldest son Wilhelm had become leading figures) were roused by the British monarch's arrival at such a sensitive time. But Victoria surged through German protest and British doubts like one of her own ironclads among lesser vessels. Nothing, and certainly not a Prussian politician or her own impudent Prussian grandson, would be allowed to stand in her way. On the way, she had her second meeting with Franz Josef, the Austrian Emperor, and in Berlin she met Bismarck, who had been raised to the German rank of Fürst or non-royal prince. Both were more impressed than they had expected to be. But her purpose was to see her daughter and son-in-law: in his case for the last time. On 15 June, Fritz died, and Victoria's grandson, Bismarck's pupil (soon to abandon his tutor) and

'Willy' to the family, became Emperor. From now on, the awfulness of Willy, his disgraceful treatment of his mother, his sense of jealous rivalry with Great Britain, his conceit, and his patronising attitude to his uncle, the Prince of Wales, became a constant source of vexation and concern to Victoria.

Another testing time came in 1891, when, once again, Bertie's involvement in the more dubious aspects of high society resulted in a court case and vast newspaper coverage. The so-called 'Tranby Croft Scandal' occurred when the Prince was playing baccarat with friends at the country house of that name. One of the players, Sir William Gordon Cumming, was accused of cheating, though it seems possible that there had been a misunderstanding of the rules. At Bertie's insistence, he promised never to play cards for money again, and the matter was closed. News of it soon was rumoured about, and Cumming brought a lawsuit in an unsuccessful attempt to clear his name. The Prince of Wales was compelled to appear as a witness. Though he had committed no impropriety himself, the details of heavy drinking and gambling that were revealed again thrust him into a lurid light. The case was publicised all over the world. A German newspaper suggested that the Prince's motto should be changed from Ich Dien ['I serve'] to Ich deal. Kaiser Wilhelm could elaborately deplore his disreputable uncle. The Queen took the affair with stoicism and expressed her support for her son. Her opinions on gambling and the high life were unchanged, but she hoped that the affair might have a beneficial effect in sobering 'Society' down somewhat.

Further strains came in 1892, when a general election dismissed Lord Salisbury and the Conservatives, and brought back not only the Liberals but Mr Gladstone, still bent on Home Rule for Ireland and now with a Commons majority to back him up. Victoria, ever conscious of her role in maintaining the unity of a triple kingdom, found the popular verdict hard to adjust to.

> 'These are trying moments & seems to me a defect in
> our much-famed Constitution, to have to part with an

admirable Govt. like Lord Salisbury's for no question of any importance, or any particular reason, merely on account of the number of votes.'

Once again partiality poked its hoof through the hem of monarchy, when the Court Circular announced that she had received the government's resignation 'with great regret'. At Gladstone's first audience as Premier, he and she were both leaning on sticks, but there was no breaking of the ice. He called his audiences with her a 'form' and a 'sham'; she used almost identical words, 'a farce and a form'; to her he remained 'the really wicked GOM'. They simply did not discuss controversial issues at all. She flatly refused to agree to the radical and openly anti-royalist Henry Labouchere being in the Cabinet, and called her new ministers 'a motley crew'. The Home Rule Bill passed its third reading in the Commons on 2 September, with a majority of thirty-four. The House of Lords threw it out by a vote of four hundred and nineteen to forty-one. That ended the matter, within the Palace of Westminster at least, for fifteen years. The Queen was pleased but not surprised. Gladstone's government lived on until early 1894, harassed by imperial-minded demands to strengthen the Royal Navy, while he dreamed of abolishing or taming the House of Lords. At last, aged 84, he announced to her his intention to resign at the end of that Parliamentary session, a piece of news which he hoped might unleash some regret, or statement of gratitude – some acknowledgement of sixty-one years of public service. She said nothing of the sort. In the letter, which acknowledged his formal letter of resignation, she wished him a peaceful future, and ended, 'The Queen would gladly have conferred a peerage on Mr Gladstone, but she knows that he would not accept it.'

She was glad and happy to see the back of him. Gladstone, his reverence for monarchy unshaken, felt injured and offended at her cold and offhand treatment, and famously compared himself to a Sicilian mule he had ridden on a journey long before.

'I had been on the back of the beast for many scores of hours. It had done me no wrong. It had rendered me much valuable service. But ... I could not get up the smallest shred of feeling for the brute. I could neither love nor like it.'

As far as the Queen was concerned, he was correct only in the last sentence. Victoria did not feel that he had done no wrong, and any valuable service was so far back in the past as to be forgotten. She had railed against him to her confidants now for decades. But there was one short and happier coda for him. In 1897, Gladstone and the Queen met when both were on holiday at Cannes and ' ... she gave me her hand ... which had never before happened with me during all my life.' But her views had not changed, nor even softened. In 1898, when he died, she remarked, 'How can I say I am sorry when I am not?' She was angry with the Prince of Wales for being one of the pallbearers at the funeral, but Bertie and Alix had always remained on good personal terms with Gladstone.

By 1890 and despite his string of extramarital liaisons, Bertie was a well-established paterfamilias, with two sons and three daughters. He, too, had done his duty by the succession, and his eldest son, Albert Victor, known to the family as 'Eddy', became engaged at the end of 1891 to an Anglo-German princess, May, daughter of the Duke of Teck, and herself a granddaughter of George III. But within six weeks, Eddy was dead, carried off by pneumonia. Eddy had not been promising regal material – dull, languid, easily impressionable, though good-natured enough – and even his family could not think of the untimely death of 'poor, dear Eddy' as a national calamity. His younger brother, George, was a more robust and steady character, and after a respectable interval, Princess May found herself again engaged to the second in line to the throne. 'Georgie' had hoped to marry his first cousin, Marie, daughter of his Uncle Alfred and his Russian wife, but she had declined. (As Queen Mary, May of Teck would live to see her grand-daughter

Elizabeth II become Queen in 1952.) In Victoria's estimation, George's star rose with his new eminence: 'I think dear Georgie so nice, sensible & truly right-minded, & so anxious to improve himself.' When his first child was born, a son, in June 1894, she noted with satisfaction that for the first time in English history, the monarch had three living generations of direct heirs. For the great-grandmother, it was a great relief to see in Bertie's heir the sense of duty and firmness of character that she felt was indispensable for the preservation of the monarchy. In 1892 she had learned, with some surprise, that for six years, governments of both parties had been keeping the Prince of Wales personally informed of Cabinet decisions. Twenty years earlier this discovery would have created a massive row, but now, after some protest and a demand for the practice to stop, the Queen acquiesced.

When Victoria accepted Gladstone's resignation in 1894, she did not ask for his advice on a successor, but sent for Lord Rosebery, a Scottish peer who had been Gladstone's Foreign Secretary. She might equally well, and was more widely expected to, have sent for Sir William Harcourt, the other strong candidate. But she did not like Harcourt, and while she distrusted the Liberal Party and its policies, she liked Rosebery and believed with some justification that he would be less Gladstonian in his politics. Her main reservation about him was that he was too clever, and she wrote to him before he became Premier that 'Lord Rosebery is so clever that he may be carried away by a sense of humour, which is a little dangerous.' Under Rosebery, Home Rule was dropped from the Liberal agenda, but Harcourt as Chancellor of the Exchequer introduced death duties, much to the Queen's dislike, but as a 'money Bill' the Lords could not prevent it. The government would not abandon the Liberal quest to reform the House of Lords, which had emerged as a solid bastion of Conservatism, able and willing to defeat any constitutional change of which it disapproved, however big the elected majority in the Commons. Victoria, with some reluctance, accepted that there was a case for 'reconstruction', but she was also in touch with Lord Salisbury, for whom the Lords' Tory majority was not likely to be a problem. She sent him a 'Very Private' question, as to whether his party was ready for a general election. Even in her mid-seventies, with the twentieth century a few years away, she was pushing past the limits of her 'above politics' status in the hope of securing the election of the government of her wishes. By this time, the torch of anti-monarchism had been handed on to a new generation of activists. In 1894, when the Queen's great-grandson Albert Edward was born (the future Edward VIII), the pioneer Labour politician Keir Hardie noted that there had also occurred the assassination of the French President, Carnot, and a major disaster at a Welsh colliery, in which 251 miners were killed. The House of Commons congratulated Prince George and Princess May, sent its commiserations to the French people, and ignored the Welsh miners. To Hardie ...

> '... the life of one Welsh miner is of greater commercial and moral value to the British nation than the whole Royal crowd put together, from the Royal Great-Grandmama down to the puling Royal Great-Grandchild.'

But as his party grew, it became as staunchly monarchist as the others – there was no appetite among the mass of its supporters for an end to monarchy in Britain. In June 1895, Rosebery's government was defeated in the Commons, and the Queen summoned Salisbury again as Prime Minister. A general election that year confirmed the Conservatives in power, with a large majority. But though Victoria respected the Olympian Salisbury, she rather missed Rosebery: '... personally I am vy fond of Ld Rosebery & prefer him (though not his Politics) to Ld. S. – he is so much attached to me personally.'

Lord Salisbury's politics were above royal reproach, especially the dynamic imperialism of his Colonial Secretary, the one-time republican Radical Joseph Chamberlain. Imperial

Britain was still collecting possessions, putting down tribes, and asserting itself against other imperialist powers, especially Germany. The Kaiser's policy was so blatantly anti-British that he was for several years not persona grata in London. On 23 September 1896, the Queen reached a milestone in her career that greatly pleased her. 'Today is the day on which I have reigned longer, by a day, than any English sovereign.' There were many congratulations but no special festivities. Great things were, however, being planned for the following year, her Diamond Jubilee.

In June 1897, the seventy-eight-year-old Queen participated with her people in the celebrations. On 21 June, she came to London for a service of thanksgiving in St Paul's Cathedral. But she declared herself too infirm to get up the steps, and so remained outside. 'After 60 years' reign, to thank God in the Street!!!' commented one continental relative. But God sent sunshine and the Queen basked in such a tide of adulation as no British monarch had experienced before. She had survived into the modern, technological world that had been emerging throughout her reign. An electric current had carried her telegraph message to her peoples round the world: 'From my heart I thank my beloved people. May God bless them!' Electric lights shone in the decorations, and officials could check by telephone on the progress of her procession through the crowd-lined streets. A cinematograph film jerkily captured the movements of the guests arriving at St Paul's. Underground railways helped bring the crowds to line the procession. As darkness fell, bonfires blazed around London and throughout Britain. Steam and electricity drove the presses that turned out tributes, Jubilee supplements and portraits of the Queen by the million.

If the Queen was the focus of events and attention, the Empire was the theme of her Jubilee. For the first time it could present itself as a family of nations, with top-hatted premiers from Canada, New Zealand and Australia joining with the more splendidly attired royalties of India. And London, the imperial capital, was also celebrating itself – the new buildings, the monuments, the bustling traffic, all the signs of conspicuous wealth, which seemed to confirm its status as the biggest city in the world as well as the centre of its greatest Empire.

> 'No one ever, I believe, has met with such an ovation as was given to me, passing through those six miles of streets ... the crowds were quite indescribable, and their enthusiasm truly marvellous and deeply touching. The cheering was quite deafening, and every face seemed to be filled with real joy.'

So wrote the Queen in her diary after the extraordinary day. Signs of old age and physical deterioration were gradually accumulating. The wheelchair was used more and more often. The Queen's eyesight was also beginning to fail, and she found small print and small writing difficult to read. Her own writing became exaggeratedly large. In May 1899, she made what would be her last trip abroad, to her favourite resort, Cimiez on the French Riviera. Later that year, war resumed in South Africa. The Second Boer War opened with a string of British failures and rebuffs, much to the distress of the Queen. Like many others, she was of the opinion that second-rate generals had been sent out to lead her indomitable soldiers. She wanted to see Roberts and Kitchener (whose victory the previous year at Omdurman in the Sudan had at last, in her eyes, avenged Gordon) sent out. But her distress was not for the public to know, and Mr Balfour, Leader of the Commons, was ringingly informed on one visit, 'Please understand that there is no one depressed in this house; we are not interested in the possibilities of defeat; they do not exist.' By 1900, partly through practices and policies that would certainly be considered war crimes today, British forces gained the ascendancy and the tide of war turned. In this year, the Queen made another visit to Ireland, where she had not been for almost forty years. Her willingness to go had been prompted by the participation of Irish troops in the Boer War, in much greater numbers than the Irish Brigade on the Boer side. It was a lengthy stay for her, just over three weeks, and it passed without incident, but under firm policing. Loyalist demonstrations were encouraged, nationalist ones kept back. She returned to Balmoral to celebrate her birthday and to receive a torrent of gifts and telegrams.

Back at Osborne, on 25 July, she was told that her son Alfred, since 1893 Duke of Saxe-Coburg, had an incurable illness of the throat. Only a few days later, news came that he had died, the third of her children to predecease her. That autumn she paid what was to be her last visit to Balmoral. Her health had been declining steadily through the year, in a way that was hard to define: no distinctive symptoms, but rather a general weakening. Despite this, she strove to attend to the dispatch boxes, and there was also the 'Khaki' general election in December, which saw Salisbury and his Tories and Liberal Unionists returned in what was the British public's last fling with jingoistic imperialism. The diary was still kept, though its contents lament her own feeling of weakness and fatigue. She often became drowsy in the course of the day, and her eyesight was become so dim that she could scarcely see the candles glimmering on the Christmas tree at Osborne. For the start of 1901, she noted, 'Another year begun & I am feeling so weak and unwell that I enter upon it sadly.' Her formidable constitution was giving up. On 6 January she wrote to Vicky, now the Dowager Empress Frederick, that she hoped soon to improve, but as January wore on it was plain to those around her that Victoria had not long to live. The letter to Vicky was her last one, and after the 13 January she made no more entries in the long-kept diary. The weather was grey and overcast, but she was still going out each day in her pony-chaise, until on 17 January the gradual ebbing of energy and strength took a sharper downwards turn, and her surviving children were sent for. The Queen's illness was officially announced, and regular bulletins were issued.

Prince Arthur had been in Berlin when he was sent for,

and his cousin Kaiser Wilhelm came to Osborne with him. Randall Davidson, now Bishop of Winchester, whose diocese included the Isle of Wight, came to join the local vicar. As the two clergymen prayed in her room, the Queen lay unresponsive until Davidson recalled that her favourite hymn (though written by the 'romaniser' J F Newman) was 'Lead Kindly Light'. As he recited the words, he saw that she was conscious and listening. Though she had often shown an almost-morbid interest in the deaths of other people, Victoria had deplored the idea of dying with the family assembled round her. Nevertheless, as her own last moments became imminent, her children gathered round the bed, with their cousin the Kaiser. It was he, with his good arm, and Dr Reid, who supported her pillow through the final two and a half hours of life. Victoria did not speak. Her last recorded word had been earlier that day, when the Prince of Wales had bent over her, and she had whispered, 'Bertie'. Just after six-thirty, on 21 January, she died.

The Queen had set down, with typical attention to detail, the arrangements for her own funeral. After ten days lying in state at Osborne, her coffin was taken to Gosport, then by train to London for her last procession through a purple-draped capital, and finally to Windsor. On 4 February she was buried beside Albert in the mausoleum she had commissioned in 1861.

To everyone, her death seemed to signify the close of an era, a feeling intensified by its proximity to the end of the nineteenth century. The adjective 'Victorian', which had been used to denote her epoch as early as 1875, originally with a sense of 'modern', very soon came into general usage to describe and demarcate the recent past. It would not be long, after the first shock of the news, and the early saccharine tributes, before a note of criticism crept into some of the obituary comments. But the Queen's reputation held up remarkably well. Even the notorious debunker of great Victorian reputations, Lytton Strachey, could not puncture that of Victoria herself. Like the Queen's person, her reputation was both expansive and solid. Any number of pins could be stuck in it without doing real damage or reaching a sensitive part. Her own frankness in *Leaves* had partly seen to that. Now, although Princess Beatrice, as 'editor' of her mother's diaries, would burn many pages in a fit of loyal embarrassment, it was the feeling among many people that they 'knew' the Queen that kept her memory green. For them it was not the crabbed, hidden 'widow of Windsor' that had died, but the mellow, visible, matriarchal Queen-Empress, before whom courtiers and kaisers trembled, but who enjoyed taking her tea and gleaning parish news in the back-kitchen of a Highland cottage.

For a great symbol of enduring stability, it was remarkable what changes she had undergone. At the start of her reign, she was seen as more German than English, a member of a foreign dynasty that happened to be Britain's royal family. By the end, Britain and Germany were unfriendly rivals and she was identified as wholly British. Then there was the progression from Liberal to Conservative sympathies. Among historians, debate would go on for decades about whether she was a 'good thing' or a 'bad thing'. As details of her numerous forays into the grey areas of constitutional behaviour, and even beyond, gradually became known, so her political influence and effectiveness was realised and analysed. In the 1930s, this resulted in a wordy war between Liberal historians who resented her treatment of Gladstone and felt her to have been an obstacle to progress; and their Conservative colleagues, some of whom went as far as to say that the country would have been better-governed if she had ruled, like a continental monarch, without a Parliament at all, rather than merely reigned, having to accept much of what she disapproved of. More than a century after her death, her forceful personality, her personal story, her presence at the centre of events for so long, her courage, her obstinacy, still make her a puzzle to biographers and readers. An ardent anti-royalist could write about her as a vastly rich, greedy and self-centred woman whose prime concern was always to maintain her own position and whose social concerns were trivial and cosmetic. Yes, she complained, via her Private Secretary, to the mayor of Windsor about the wretched state of the town's housing for the poor, so near her great castle – but did she throw open the doors of Windsor Castle to the paupers and jobless? Most assuredly not. But it would not be a complete or wholly honest account of a woman who, of quite commonplace disposition and interests, but with an uncommon will and equally rare sense of duty, found herself at the age of eighteen in a position of unique social and political importance, and held it through bad times without ever quite collapsing and through better times in triumph, for more than sixty years. She was frequently shown great forbearance, by her family, by politicians, and by the British people, but no one was forced to attend her Jubilees, or to wait in the rain to see her train run past at its steady forty miles an hour. People did these things because Queen Victoria meant something to them, and they found her worthy of that 'something', in which patriotism, personal loyalty, attachment to national tradition, and often something akin to love, all were present. If much of that public love and veneration went into the Queen's well-packed coffin, along with many of her personal knick-knacks and mementoes, enough was left to shed a certain lustre on Bertie when at the age of sixty, he became king Edward VII.

At the time when that transition took place, out in the far Hebrides the weather was stormy, so wild that for eleven days no boat could land on the little Isle of Eriskay. When one eventually arrived with the postbag, the parish priest, Father Allan Macdonald, overheard a typically allusive conversation in Gaelic between a boatman and some bystanders on the jetty.

'The Old Woman's gone.'
'What Old Woman?'
'The Old Woman Herself.'
'What herself?'
'The Old Woman that's at the Steering.'
'Och, has she gone, at last?'

They were perhaps the last of her subjects in Great Britain to learn of the death of Queen Victoria.

Queen Victoria photographed for her Diamond Jubilee, 1897.

Queen Victoria receiving the sacrament at her coronation, 1837.

Princess Victoria, c.1837.

Right: Queen Victoria and Albert, 1840.

Below: Queen Victoria and Albert's wedding, St James's Palace.

Assassination attempt by Edward Oxford in 1840.

Some of Queen Victoria's Prime Ministers *(clockwise from top left)*: Melbourne, Disraeli, Gladstone, Palmerston.

Poverty persisted under Queen Victoria's reign *(above)*, while engineering achievements and technology advanced tremendously, showcased in the Great Exhibition of 1851 *(below)*.

Queen Victoria arriving at St Paul's Cathedral for her Diamond Jubilee.

Queen Victoria and some of her great-grandchildren (*left to right*): Princess Victoria, Prince Albert, Prince Edward, Prince Henry.

Queen Victoria pictured with John Brown, 1863.

Munshi Abdul Karim, attending the Queen in 1893.

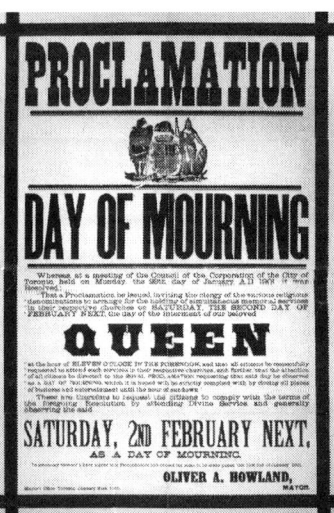

The end of an era. Queen Victoria's death in 1901 was mourned around the British Empire.

Left: Poster proclaiming February 2, 1901, as a Day of Mourning in Toronto, Ontario, Canada.

Queen Victoria: Important Dates

1819
- On 24 May, a daughter, Alexandrina Victoria is born to Edward, Duke of Kent (fourth son of George III) and Victoria Maria Louisa, daughter of the Duke of Saxe-Coburg, at Kensington Palace, London. The baby princess is fifth in line to the British throne.
- On 24 June, Victoria is christened by the Archbishop of Canterbury at Kensington Palace.
- On 16 August, eleven people are killed by troops at radical meeting at St Peter's Fields, Manchester in what became known as the 'Peterloo Massacre'.

1820
- On 23 January, Victoria's father, Edward, Duke of Kent dies at Sidmouth in Devon. Victoria is now fourth in line to the throne.
- On 29 January, King George III dies and is succeeded by his son George IV. Victoria is now third in line to the throne.
- On 23 February, members of the 'the Cato Street conspiracy', who were planning to assassinate members of the cabinet, are arrested; five are executed on 1 May.

1824
- Fraulein Louise Lehzen (always known as 'Lehzen') becomes governess to the five-year-old Princess Victoria.

- On 5 March, the First Burma war breaks out between the British and the Burmese Empire over the control of Northeastern India.

1827
- On 5 January, Victoria's uncle, Frederick, Duke of York, dies. Victoria is now second in line to the throne.
- On 20 October, during the Greek War of Independence (1821–32), British and Allied fleets destroy the Turkish navy at the Battle of Navarino.

1830
- On 26 June, King George IV dies and is succeeded by his brother William IV. Victoria is now heir to the British throne.
- On 15 September, the Liverpool and Manchester Railway opens – the first railway driven by steam power.
- In November, the Whig Earl Grey becomes Prime Minister.

1831
- On 21 July, Victoria's uncle, Leopold (her mother's brother) becomes the King of the Belgians.
- On 27 September, HMS *Beagle* begins a five-year circumnavigation of the world, for survey and scientific purposes with Charles Darwin aboard.

1832
- Between 1832 and 1835, Victoria takes part in a series of tours of England and Wales organised

- by her mother, much to the disapproval of King William IV.
- After the resistance of the Lords to the Act is ended, the First Reform Act becomes law.

1836
- In April 1836, Victoria's Saxe-Coburg cousins, Ernest and Albert, are invited to Kensington Palace for Victoria's seventeenth birthday celebrations.
- Thomas Lister is appointed as the first Registrar General for England and Wales, to head the new General Register Office.
- Civil marriage is made legal in the Marriage Act of 1836.

1837
- On 24 May, Victoria turns eighteen, which means she will no longer need a Regent (her mother) to rule on her behalf when she becomes Queen.
- On 20 June, King William IV dies without any children and the young princess becomes Queen Victoria.
- On 20 July, London's first inter-city railway station opens at Euston Square with completion of London and Birmingham Railway.
- Charles Dickens' first novel, *The Pickwick Papers*, first written for publication as a serial, is published in book form.

1838
- In May, Chartists publish *The People's Charter* 'being the outline of an Act to provide for the just representation of the people of Great Britain'.
- On 28 June, Queen Victoria is crowned at Westminster Abbey. More than 400,000 people line the streets hoping to see the young queen.
- William Henry Fox Talbot, scientist, inventor and photography pioneer, succeeds in making photographic prints on silver chloride paper.

1839
- In February, Victoria accuses Lady Flora Hastings, one of her mother's ladies in waiting who she dislikes intensely, of being pregnant by Sir John Conroy, her mother's partner, who she also dislikes. When it is revealed that Lady Flora's enlarged stomach is due to a tumour, Victoria loses some of her popularity.
- On 7 May, in what became known as the 'Bedchamber Crisis' the Prime Minister, Lord Melbourne, who has closely advised Victoria since her accession, resigns. He suggests to Victoria that she appoint the Tory Lord Peel as new Prime Minister. Peel requests that Victoria replace some of her Whig Ladies of the Bedchamber with Tory Ladies. When Victoria refuses he declines to accept the position of Prime Minister. Melbourne returns as Prime Minister fuelling claims that he and Victoria were too close.
- On 15 October, Queen Victoria

asks her cousin, Prince Albert of Saxe-Coburg and Gotha, to marry her and he accepts.
- On 25 October, Bradshaw's *Railway Companion*, consisting of Railway Time Tables and Assistant to Railway Travelling, is published.

1840
- On 6 February, Prince Albert is granted the British title of Royal Highness.
- On 10 February, Queen Victoria marries Prince Albert in the Chapel Royal at St James's Palace.
- On 22 May, transportation of convicts to New South Wales is ended.
- On 10 June, Edward Oxford tries to assassinate the Queen as she and Prince Albert were travelling in an open carriage down Constitution Hill. He is caught by spectators and handed over to the police. He is later found guilty but insane.
- On 21 November, Queen Victoria's first child is born at Buckingham Palace, a daughter called Victoria who is to be known as 'The Princess Royal'.
- The Opium War with China begins.

1841
- On 9 November, Queen Victoria gives birth to a son, Albert Edward ('Bertie').
- On 30 August, Prime Minister Melbourne resigns; Robert Peel becomes Prime Minister.

1842
- On 29 May, both Queen Victoria and Prince Albert see a man pointing a pistol at their carriage while they are driving back to Buckingham Palace but he is not caught.
- On 30 May, the Queen sets out for another drive, to Hampstead and back, with the intention of giving the man a chance to try again. A gun is fired and John Francis is seized. He is transported to Australia.
- On 3 July, another assassination attempt is made on Queen Victoria's life when John Bean shoots at her from a London crowd. He is sent to prison for eighteen months.
- In September, Lehzen retires and goes to stay with her sister in Germany.
- In the autumn, Queen Victoria and Prince Albert make their first visit to Scotland.
- On 17 August, the Opium War comes to an end with the Treaty of Nanking.

1843
- On 25 April, Queen Victoria gives birth to her second daughter, Alice Maud Mary, at Buckingham Palace.
- On 19 July, Brunel's first ocean-going iron steamship, SS *Great Britain*, is launched at Bristol.
- On 5 September, Queen Victoria and Prince Albert meet King Louis Philippe and Queen

Marie Amelie at Château d'Eu in Normandy during a visit to France.
- On 6 April, William Wordsworth is appointed poet laureate.

1844
- On 6 June, Sir George Williams founds the Young Men's Christian Association (YMCA) in London, now the oldest and largest youth charity in the world.
- On 6 August, a second son, Alfred Ernest Albert, is born to Queen Victoria and Prince Albert at Buckingham Palace.
- On 21 December, the first co-operative store is opened by the *Rochdale* Society of Equitable Pioneers.

1845
- Queen Victoria and Prince Albert buy Osborne House on the Isle of Wight.
- Friedrich Engels' *The Condition of the Working Class in England* is published in German. The first authorised English edition is published in 1892.

1846
- In January, Prince Albert attends a House of Commons debate on the repeal of the Corn Laws as an observer and is fiercely criticised for doing so by the Tory leader, Lord George Bentinck.
- On 23 May, a third daughter, Helena Augusta Victoria ('Lenchen'), is born to Queen Victoria and Prince Albert at Buckingham Palace.
- On 29 June, Robert Peel resigns as Prime Minister after failing to gain support for a repeal of the Corn Laws. Whig Lord John Russell takes over as Prime Minister.

1847
- The Factory Act or Ten Hour Act establishes a ten-hour working day.
- On 26 August, the Conservatives win the General Election and Whig Lord John Russell remained as Prime Minister.
- A silver crown is introduced with a medieval style Gothic portrait of Queen Victoria on it.

1848
- Queen Victoria and Prince Albert buy the lease of Balmoral House in Royal Deeside in Scotland.
- On 18 March, a fourth daughter, Louise Caroline Alberta, is born to Queen Victoria and Prince Albert at Buckingham Palace.
- Britain annexes land between the Orange and Vaal Rivers in South Africa and the region is proclaimed as the Orange River Sovereignty.

1849
- On 13 May, there is another failed assassination attempt against the Queen. William Hamilton shoots at the Queen as she rides in her carriage with three of her children and her maid, Annie Macdonald. He is arrested and pleads guilty,

and is sentenced to seven years transportation, arriving in Fremantle in 1854 before fading into obscurity.
- In August, Queen Victoria and Prince Albert make a successful state visit to Ireland.
- The Board of Inland Revenue is established under the Inland Revenue Board Act.
- Cockfighting and bull-baiting are banned.

1850
- On 1 May, a third son, Arthur William Patrick Albert, is born to Queen Victoria and Prince Albert at Buckingham Palace.
- On 27 June, Robert Pate runs up to the carriage in which the Queen is travelling and hits her hard on the head with the brass head of a cane. He is arrested at the scene and charged with assaulting the Queen. He is found guilty and sentenced to transportation for seven years.
- On 29 September, by the bull *Universalis Ecclesiae*, Pope Pius IX recreates the Roman Catholic diocesan hierarchy in England.
- On 31 March, RMS *Royal Adelaide*, a paddle steamship, is wrecked off Margate and as many as 400 lives are lost.

1851
- On 1 May, the Great Exhibition at Crystal Palace in London is opened by the Queen to celebrate art, science, trade, and industry. It marks one of the high points in Victoria's reign. Its great success is in the main thanks to the enthusiasm and hard work of Prince Albert, who took up the idea for such an exhibition and made it his own. More than six million entry tickets are sold.
- In December, Lord Palmerston is dismissed as Foreign Secretary for unauthorised recognition of the self-coup d'état staged by Prince Louis-Napoleon Bonaparte in France.
- In August, the first telegraph cable is laid across the English Channel.
- The Reuters Telegram Company is founded by Paul Julius Reuter in London.

1852
- In June, Edward Stanley, Earl of Derby, wins the general election and becomes Prime Minister of a Conservative government.
- On 19 December, the Conservative government collapses when the House of Commons fails to pass the Chancellor's budget. George Gordon, Earl of Aberdeen, becomes Prime Minister of a Peelite-Whig Coalition.
- Queen Victoria and Prince Albert purchase Balmoral House outright for £31,500. Prince Albert sets about designing and arranging for the building of an entirely new castle at Balmoral to replace the small Balmoral House.

1853

- On 7 April, the Queen's fourth son, Leopold George Duncan Albert, is born at Buckingham Palace.
- On 28 September, the Queen lays the foundation stone for Balmoral Castle.
- On 29 March, Manchester receives city status.
- On 5 October, the Crimean War (1853–1856) begins.

1854

- In the Crimean War, the following battles take place: the Battle of the Alma; the Battle of Balaclava and the Charge of the Light Brigade; and the Battle of Inkerman.
- Around this time, cigarettes are introduced in England.

1855

- On 30 January, George Gordon, Earl of Aberdeen and Prime Minister, resigns over the investigation into the Crimean War.
- On 6 February, Henry Temple, Lord Palmerston, takes over as Prime Minister of a minority government after George Gordon resigns.
- In April, Napoleon Bonaparte's great-nephew, the self-appointed Emperor Napoleon III, and his wife, the Empress Eugénie, visit the Queen at Windsor Castle at the suggestion of Prince Albert. Their state visit lasts a week.
- In August, Queen Victoria, Prince Albert and the couple's two eldest children, Victoria and Albert Edward (later King Edward VII), enjoy a ten-day state visit to Paris.
- In autumn, Queen Victoria and Prince Albert and members of the royal family are able to stay in Balmoral Castle for the first time.

1856

- On 30 March, the Treaty of Paris ends the Crimean War.
- The Victoria Cross is introduced by Queen Victoria as prime decoration for valour.
- Balmoral Castle is completed and the old Balmoral House is demolished.
- A patent is taken out on the Bessemer process (the first inexpensive industrial process for the mass production of steel) by its inventor, Henry Bessemer.

1857

- On 14 April, a fifth daughter, Beatrice Mary Victoria Feodore, is born to Queen Victoria and Prince Albert at Buckingham Palace. She is the last of Queen Victoria and Prince Albert's nine children.
- On 25 June, Prince Albert is granted the title Prince Consort.
- On 10 May, the Indian Mutiny (1857–1858) breaks out.
- The Second Opium War (1856–1860) with China is precipitated by the Chinese boarding of a British-registered ship suspected of piracy (the *Arrow*).

Queen Victoria: Important Dates

1858
- On 20 February, Edward Stanley, Earl of Derby becomes Prime Minister of a Conservative government when the Whig government collapsed.
- On 25 January, Queen Victoria's daughter, Princess Victoria, marries Prince Frederick of Prussia at the Chapel Royal, St James's Palace, London.
- On 18 June, the Indian Mutiny is brought to an end at the Battle of Gwalior.

1859
- On 12 June, Henry Temple, Viscount Palmerston wins the General Election and becomes Prime Minister of a Liberal government.
- William Rathbone introduces district nursing.

1861
- On 16 March, Queen Victoria's mother and Prince Albert's aunt, the Duchess of Kent, dies at Frogmore House, Windsor at the age of seventy-four.
- On 22 August, Queen Victoria and Prince Albert embark on an eight-day visit to Ireland. Prince Albert goes to the Curragh to watch a military review in which his nineteen-year-old heir, Prince Albert Edward (Bertie), is taking part.
- In September, Bertie disgraces himself by having a liaison with an Irish actress, Nellie Clifton.
- On 1 October, Mrs Beeton's *Book of Household Management* is published.
- On 14 December, Prince Albert dies of typhoid fever. Queen Victoria is devastated by his death.
- On 23 December, a funeral is held for Prince Albert. His remains are moved to St George's Chapel in Windsor Castle, before being taken to the new Mausoleum at Frogmore in December 1862.

1862
- A profound grief afflicts Victoria now and for a decade to come.
- In May, Queen Victoria retreats to Balmoral.
- On 5 September, Henry Coxwell reaches a height of over seven miles in an air balloon.
- On 1 July, Queen Victoria's daughter, Princess Alice, marries Louis IV, Grand Duke of Hesse-Darmstadt and the Rhine at Osborne House on the Isle of Wight.
- Late in the year, Victoria visits Coburg in Germany, the first of three visits in the course of the next three years. She visits King Leopold on her way and calls on Lehzen, now a Baroness.

1863
- Between 1862 and 1876 Sir Gilbert Scott and a team of craftsmen work on the Albert Memorial.
- On 10 March, Queen Victoria's son, Prince Albert Edward, marries Alexandra, daughter of

Christian IX, King of Denmark at St George's Chapel, Windsor.
- On a second visit to Germany, Queen Victoria has a short meeting with the Austrian Emperor, Franz Josef.
- On 18 December, the world's first electric underground railway, called the Metropolitan, opens in London.

1864
- Queen Victoria presses her ministers not to intervene in the Prussia–Denmark War.
- On 28 September, the International Working Men's Association is founded in London.

1865
- On a third visit to Germany, Queen Victoria unveils a statue of Albert in the marketplace in Coburg.
- On 29 October, John Russell takes over as Prime Minister when Henry Temple, Viscount Palmerston dies while in office.

1866
- On 5 July, Queen Victoria's daughter, Princess Helena, marries Christian, Prince of Schleswig-Holstein-Sonderburg-Augustenburg at Windsor Castle.
- Queen Victoria attends the State Opening of Parliament, her first public appearance since the death of Prince Albert.
- The Albert Medal is established as an award for gallantry in saving life.
- On 28 June, Edward Stanley, Earl of Derby takes over as Prime Minister when Russell's Liberal government collapses.

1867
- Work starts on the Royal Albert Hall.
- The Second Reform Act is passed, doubling the electorate to over two million.

1868
- Queen Victoria publishes *Leaves from the Journal of Our Life in the Highlands*.
- On 27 February, Benjamin Disraeli takes over as Prime Minister when Edward Stanley, Earl of Derby, resigns due to ill health.
- On 3 December, William Gladstone is elected Prime Minister of a Liberal government.
- On 26 May, Michael Barrett is the last man to be publicly hanged in England.

1871
- Trade unions are given legal status with the adoption of the Trade Union Act.
- On 21 March, Queen Victoria's daughter, Louise, marries John Campbell, Marquess of Lorne at St George's Chapel, Windsor.
- On 29 March, the Royal Albert Hall is opened by Queen Victoria. She is so overcome by emotion that the Prince of Wales has to speak in her place.
- On 13 July, the first cat show in England takes place in the Crystal Palace in London.

1872

- On 29 February, as Queen Victoria is about to alight from her carriage inside the grounds of Buckingham Palace, John O'Connor runs up to the carriage and aims a pistol at her head. He had hoped to force the Queen to free all Fenian prisoners, but he is foiled by John Brown who hands him over to the police. Although it is later determined the pistol was not loaded, he is charged with treason and pleads guilty. He is sentenced to a year in prison and twenty strokes with a birch rod.
- The Ballot Act establishes secret voting.
- Joseph Arch founds the National Agricultural Labourers' Union.

1873

- Queen Victoria is persuaded by the government to welcome the Shah of Persia as her guest.
- On 24 May, Alexandra Palace and Park is opened by the renowned landscape architect, Alexander McKenzie, as a pioneering Victorian leisure park and acentre for education and entertainment. Following a fire some two weeks later, it has to be rebuilt and re-opens in 1875.

1874

- On 23 January, Queen Victoria's son, Prince Alfred, marries Maria Alexandrovna, daughter of Tsar Alexander II of Russia, in the Grand Church of the Winter Palace, St Petersburg, Russia.
- On 20 February, Benjamin Disraeli wins the general election and becomes Prime Minister of a Conservative government.
- Joseph Arch leads a farm workers' strike.

1875

- On 14 December, Queen Victoria's daughter, Alice of Hesse, dies of diphtheria.
- Founding of Mason College in Birmingham (later becomes Birmingham University).
- An English Hockey Association is founded.

1876

- On 1 May, Queen Victoria is declared Empress of India.
- British Prime Minister Benjamin Disraeli buys Egypt's shareholding in the Suez Canal for £4 million.
- Grey squirrels are introduced from North America and they begin to oust native red squirrels.

1877

- On 1 January, Queen Victoria's new title, Empress of India, is proclaimed at the Delhi Durbar, an Indian imperial style mass assembly organised by the British at Coronation Park, Delhi, India, to mark the succession of an Emperor or Empress of India.
- The 'Cleopatra's Needle' obelisk is transported from Egypt to London.
- Red Cross forms the Ambulance Association, later St John's Ambulance Brigade.

1878
- On 14 December, Queen Victoria's daughter, Alice, Grand Duchess of Hesse-Darmstadt dies.
- On 11 November, the City and Guilds of London Institute is founded.

1879
- On 13 March, Queen Victoria's son, Prince Arthur, marries Princess Louise Margaret, daughter of Prince Frederick of Prussia, at St George's Chapel, Windsor.
- The Anglo–Zulu War (11 January–4 July) takes place in South Africa.
- Sir James Murray begins work on the *New* (later *Oxford*) *English Dictionary*.

1880
- In the general election, Gladstone's Liberals won 352 seats, a gain of 110, against 237 for the Conservatives and 63 for the Irish Home Rule League.
- Greenwich Mean Time established throughout the country.
- On 16 December, the First Boer War (1880–1881) begins.

1882
- On 2 March, yet another attempt to assassinate Queen Victoria fails. Roderick Maclean fires a shot at Queen Victoria as she is leaving a train and getting into a carriage to take her to Windsor. He is arrested at the scene and tried for treason. He is acquitted of the charge on the grounds of insanity but imprisoned indefinitely.
- On 19 April, Charles Darwin dies.
- On 27 April, Queen Victoria's son, Prince Leopold, marries Helena, daughter of George Victor, Prince of Waldeck-Pyrmont.

1884
- On 4 January, the Fabian Society is founded, having as its goal the establishment of a democratic socialist state in Great Britain.
- The Third Reform Act further expands electorate to include farm labourers.
- On 28 March, Queen Victoria's son, Prince Leopold, a haemophiliac, dies following an accident in Cannes, France.
- General Gordon under siege in Khartoum.

1885
- On 26 January, General Gordon is killed at Khartoum. A relief expedition arrives a few days later.
- On 23 June, Robert Gascoyne-Cecil, Marquess of Salisbury, is elected Prime Minister of a minority Conservative government.
- On 23 July, Queen Victoria's daughter, Princess Beatrice, marries Prince Henry of Battenberg at Whippingham Church, Isle of Wight.

Queen Victoria: Important Dates

1886
- On 9 January, the first goods train passes through the newly completed Severn Tunnel, linking South Gloucestershire in the west of England to Monmouthshire in south Wales.
- On 1 February, William Gladstone takes over as Prime Minister after Salisbury's minority Conservative government falls. He resigns after the defeat of the Irish Home Rule Bill.
- On 20 July, Salisbury wins the general election for the Conservatives.

1887
- On 20 June, the Golden Jubilee of Queen Victoria is celebrated on the occasion of the fiftieth anniversary of her accession to the throne on 20 June 1837. It is celebrated with a service of thanksgiving at Westminster Abbey and a banquet to which fifty European kings and princes are invited.
- On 13 November in Trafalgar Square, in what came to be known as the 'Bloody Sunday' riots, there are violent clashes between the police and demonstrators, some marching against unemployment and some against the government's handling of the Irish situation.

1890
- Britain cedes Heligoland to Germany.
- Opening of the first electric underground railway (City and South London).
- Queen Victoria appoints Crown Derby as 'Manufacturers of porcelain to Her Majesty'; Crown Derby becomes Royal Crown Derby china from now on.

1891
- The Tranby Croft affair: the Prince of Wales gives evidence in a case concerning a friend of his said to have cheated at baccarat, a card game loved by the Prince.
- Completion of New Scotland Yard building, by Norman Shaw.

1892
- On 15th August, William Gladstone wins the general election and becomes Prime Minister, for the last time, of a minority Liberal government.
- Rowton Houses, dwellings for unmarried men, is founded by Lord Rowton.
- 'Gentleman Jim' Corbett becomes first world heavyweight boxing champion.

1893
- A Royal Commission on Agricultural Depression is appointed by Queen Victoria on the recommendation of the government: it reports back in 1897.
- *The Memoirs of Sherlock Holmes*, a volume containing eleven Sherlock Holmes short stories by Arthur Conan Doyle, is published.

- A mine disaster at Combs Colliery, near Dewsbury kills 139 miners.

1894
- On 5 March, Archibald Primrose, Earl of Roseberry, takes over as Prime Minister after William Gladstone resigns.
- Parish, rural and urban district councils are established.
- Opening of the Manchester Ship Canal; also Tower Bridge, London.

1895
- Robert Gascoyne-Cecil, Marquess of Salisbury, wins the General Election and became Prime Minister of a Conservative government.
- Most severe February weather ever known in England: ice on some waters reaches 25 inches in thickness.
- Northern Union (later Rugby League) secedes from Rugby Union.

1897
- On 20 June, Queen Victoria's Diamond Jubilee marks her sixty years as Queen. It begins solemnly with a family Thanksgiving service at Windsor Castle, and further celebrations are held over the next two days including a carriage procession through the streets of London.
- On 21 July, the Prince of Wales opens the National Gallery of British Art, later the Tate Gallery, in London.
- Employers' Liability Act makes employers responsible for safety in workplaces.

1900
- On 30 July, Queen Victoria's son Alfred, Duke of Edinburgh and Duke of Saxe-Coburg and Gotha dies.

1901
- On 22 January, Queen Victoria dies at Osborne House. She is succeeded by her eldest son, Edward, who becomes Edward VII.
- On 2 February, a funeral service for Queen Victoria is held at St George's Chapel, Windsor Castle. She is buried next to Prince Albert in the Frogmore Mausoleum at Windsor Great Park.
- On 5 August, Queen Victoria's eldest daughter, Victoria, dies.

1902
- Salisbury resigns, and Arthur Balfour, Earl of Balfour, becomes Prime Minister.
- On 31 May, the Treaty of Vereeniging ends the Second Boer War (1899–1902).
- The Order of Merit is established in 1902 by Queen Victoria's son, King Edward VII, recognising distinguished service in the armed forces, science, art, literature, or for the promotion of culture. Admission into the order remains the personal gift of the British monarch.

Queen Victoria: Important Dates

1910
- On 6 May, Queen Victoria's eldest son, King Edward VII, dies. George V becomes King.
- On 1 February, the first sixty-two Labour Exchanges are opened.
- The Girl Guide Association is officially established in the UK under the leadership of Agnes Baden-Powell, Robert Baden-Powell's sister.

1923
- On 9 June, Queen Victoria's daughter, Helena, dies.
- Bonar Law resigns due to ill health and Stanley Baldwin becomes Prime Minister.
- In December, a general election returns a minority Conservative government; Labour are the second-largest party.

1939
- On 1 September, Hitler invades Poland from the west; two days later, France and Britain declares war on Germany, beginning World War Two (1939–45).
- In May, Anglo-Saxon treasure is found in a burial ship at Sutton Hoo.
- On 3 September the National Service (Armed Forces) Act imposes conscription on all males aged between eighteen and forty-one who have to register for service.
- On 3 December, Queen Victoria's daughter, Louise, Duchess of Argyll, dies.

1942
- On 16 January, Queen Victoria's son, Arthur, Duke of Connaught and Strathearn, dies.
- Between 23 October and 4 November, the second Battle of El Alamein, under General Montgomery, is fought near the western frontier of Egypt; this battle is the climax and turning point of the North African campaign of World War Two.
- The standard wartime 'national loaf' is introduced; soap rationing is introduced.
- On 2 December, the Beveridge Report on plans for post-war Britain is published.

1944
- On 10 February, the PAYE (pay as you earn) system of tax collection is introduced.
- On June 6, Operation Overlord, commonly known as D-Day, commences with the landing of 155,000 Allied troops on the beaches of Normandy in France.
- The standard wartime 'national loaf' is introduced; soap rationing is introduced.
- On 26 October, Princess Beatrice of Battenberg, the last of Queen Victoria's children, dies.

Select Bibliography

Altick, Richard D, *Victorian People and Ideas*. London, 1974

Benson, A C and Esher, Viscount (eds.), *The Letters of Queen Victoria*. London, 1908

Briggs, Asa, *Victorian People*. London, 1954

Duff, David, *Albert and Victoria*. London, 1972

Guedalla, Philip, *The Queen and Mr Gladstone*. London, 1933

Hardie, Frank, *The Political Influence of Queen Victoria*. Oxford, 1935

Longford, Elizabeth, *Victoria R.I.* London, 1964

Ponsonby, Frederick, *Recollections of Three Reigns*. London, 1951

Strachey, Lytton, *Queen Victoria*. London, 1921

Victoria, Queen, *Leaves from the Journal of Our Life in the Highlands*. London, 1869

Victoria, Queen, *More Leaves from the Journal of Our Life in the Highlands*. London, 1884

Wilson, A N, *The Victorians*. London, 2000